Madam C. J. Walker

The Making of an American Icon

Erica L. Ball

ROWMAN & LITTLEFIELD
Lanham • Boulder • New York • London

Published by Rowman & Littlefield
An imprint of The Rowman & Littlefield Publishing Group, Inc.
4501 Forbes Boulevard, Suite 200, Lanham, Maryland 20706
www.rowman.com

6 Tinworth Street, London SE11 5AL, United Kingdom

British Library Cataloguing in Publication Information Available

Library of Congress Cataloging-in-Publication Data

978-1-4422-6038-2 (cloth)
978-1-4422-6039-3 (electronic)

For my parents,

Eugene Ball, Jr.
and
Carolyn L. Ball

~

Contents

~

Preface

For the first forty years of her life, Madam C. J. Walker lived, like most black women born and raised in the years after the end of slavery, as an anonymous figure, spending decades striving to build a life for herself and her family in the midst of a nation that restrained her freedom of movement, limited her educational opportunities and wages, and denied her the full privileges of citizenship. She was one woman among millions of black women who migrated to towns and cities across the nation in search of freedom, who sought fair compensation for their labor, who created spaces for themselves and their families, and who insisted on creating their own definitions of beauty and experiencing and enjoying freedom on their own terms without acknowledgment or recognition from those outside their communities. In this sense, Madam Walker was an "everywoman" on a quest for a better life, one of countless black women who negotiated with the new forms of racism that emerged and ossified in the decades after emancipation. Only in the last fifteen years of her life did Madam Walker develop her business and her brand and transform herself into a public figure, a philanthropist, a race woman, and a celebrity, defining and redefining the parameters of these roles along the way.

At the same time, however, Madam Walker's entire life of invention and reinvention places her in the tradition of notable black figures who preceded her, people like Olaudah Equiano, Sojourner Truth, and Frederick Douglass, men and women who, born in the midst of slavery, crafted new narratives and origin stories for themselves and invested deeply in the freedom struggle.

She also has much in common with famous black men and women of her own era, people like Mary Church Terrell, Booker T. Washington, W.E.B. Du Bois, Jack Johnson, and Mary McLeod Bethune: women and men who came of age after emancipation, charted remarkable new career trajectories, and remained popular public figures despite the limits imposed upon them by Jim Crow–era racism. Of these, Madam Walker, perhaps more than any other, blended the hopes, aspirations, and achievements of various swaths of the black population, crossing various intra-racial class, gender, regional, and political lines. Moreover, Madam Walker ultimately lived, narrated, and came to represent a uniquely modern life. Despite the hardening of the color line and the violence that policed its barriers, Madam Walker dared to create, to build, to fight, and to succeed. And as she put it, it was she who promoted herself "from the washtub" to "the boardroom."

Madam Walker's success quickly transformed her into a black American "first"—the type of public figure whose life story resonated in collective black American culture and memory. Indeed, African Americans made meaning of Madam Walker's life story decades after her death in 1919, reframing interpretations of her "washtub to the boardroom" narrative to meet the political and cultural demands of each subsequent decade. In the early decades and middle of the twentieth century, black writers and editors celebrated Madam Walker as a symbol of African American achievement and the progress of the race. In the 1960s and '70s, some black Americans believed that Madam Walker *invented* the straightening comb (untrue), sold it to black women, and, in the process, taught women of African descent that in order to be beautiful, they needed to alter the texture of their hair and emulate white standards of beauty. Because of this, young African Americans often argued that Madam Walker's business enterprise represented exactly what they sought to reject in an age when the Afro, whether short-cropped or resplendent, signaled that the wearer truly understood that "Black is beautiful." By the late twentieth century, these arguments subsided. By then, many African Americans described Madam Walker as a pioneering example of black enterprise and wealth. Moreover, her story continued to resonate in the twenty-first century; YouTubers, fiction writers, and television directors found inspiration in the Madam C. J. Walker story. And in 2020, a popular television limited series repurposed her life story yet again, harnessing Madam Walker's narrative to contemporary debates over respectability politics and casting her as an exemplar of "authentic" black identity in contrast with her adversaries who, in their telling, favored physical attributes and activities that connoted closer proximity with whiteness.

Scholars, meanwhile, have largely engaged a different set of questions than the general public and entertainment industry. Led by Madam Walker's great-great-granddaughter A'Lelia Bundles, an array of scholars have detailed to the best of their ability Madam Walker's extraordinary life story and carefully assessed her impact on black women's beauty culture, noting that until her death in 1919, Madam Walker consistently and forcefully characterized her products in terms of black women's hair *health* and fought furiously against any suggestion that she was a hair *straightener*. Recent scholarship also clarifies Madam Walker's role as a pioneer in an industry that would prove to be crucial for the sustenance of twentieth-century civil rights campaigns and highlights her endeavors as a philanthropist and progressive political activist. Together, this growing body of scholarship has created a much more nuanced portrait of the woman who went by the name of Madam C. J. Walker.

And yet all of these studies, like this one, have had to rely heavily upon the tightly scripted narrative that Madam Walker created for herself as she built her business empire. Like other early twentieth-century pioneers in the beauty industry—Elizabeth Arden and Helena Rubinstein, for example—Madam Walker kept the details of her early life secret. With a keen understanding of the workings of an emergent celebrity culture, she sought to control the narrative of her life both in print and in visual terms. It is because of her efforts—what she said about herself and what she left unsaid—that so few details can be gleaned about the first four decades of her life. What we know about Madam Walker is largely what she wanted us to know: the story of her rise from obscurity as a poor, uneducated laundress named Sarah Breedlove who was born on a Louisiana plantation in the aftermath of the Civil War to a wealthy, famous woman named Madam C. J. Walker who owned her own company and dwelled in a mansion in the posh village of Irvington-on-Hudson just outside New York City. This was, as Madam Walker well knew, an extraordinary tale of self-fashioning and reinvention, an unprecedented transformation from an everywoman to an extraordinary woman.

Rather than seeking to separate the history of the woman from the carefully crafted narrative she disseminated during her meteoric rise, *Madam C. J. Walker: The Making of an American Icon* places Madam Walker's personal processes of reinvention at the center of her life story. This biography follows her from her birth in Louisiana and her early years in Mississippi through her relocation to cities like St. Louis, Denver, and Indianapolis. And it shows how with each of these moves, she refashioned herself anew. The daughter of former slaves, Madam Walker began her adult life as a single mother, a domestic worker, and a migrant in search of opportunity. Keenly attuned to emerging marketing and advertising strategies, Madam Walker went on to build a phenomenally successful business that redefined African American perceptions of beauty. Committed to African American advancement in all its forms, Madam Walker embraced emerging forms of black political and civic engagement. Ultimately, Madam C. J. Walker fashioned herself into a modern race woman.

Madam C. J. Walker: The Making of an American Icon also argues that Madam Walker ultimately created and embodied new ways of being for black women in the United States. During the last fifteen years of her life, as her hair-care enterprise expanded, Madam Walker further fashioned herself into a celebrity, a public figure with a platform to model her conceptions of freedom, political engagement, beauty, and success for others. Although scholars generally give this mantle of leadership to her daughter, Lelia Walker Robinson—whom Langston Hughes later called the "Joy Goddess of Harlem" in the 1920s—Madam C. J. Walker was certainly a celebrity in her own right during the last years of her life, one who served as an aspirational yet relatable symbol of modernity for black women in the United States. By stamping her image on a line of hair products that black women could purchase and use for themselves, by employing black women like herself to sell her eponymous products, by telling the story of her own reinvention on the lecture circuit, and by engaging in an array of community-building, philanthropic, and civil rights endeavors, Madam Walker crafted, marketed and embodied a new, modern vision of the race woman. And by the time of her death in 1919, the name and image of Madam C. J. Walker conjured up a wealth of meaning—both personal and political—for black Americans.

Finally, *Madam C. J. Walker: The Making of an American Icon* argues that Madam Walker must be understood as far more than a pioneer in the black beauty industry, or in American women's entrepreneurship, or in black philanthropy. For in addition to these characterizations, all of which are accurate, Madam Walker must be considered an American icon. Like other early twentieth-century business pioneers, Madam Walker helped to inaugurate an emerging transnational American corporate capitalism and its attendant mass consumer and celebrity cultures. Like other American icons, Madam Walker's name and image came to signify a way of being, a set of questions, and a modern political sensibility that resonated with her supporters and fans. Unlike many of her famous African American contemporaries, including educators like Booker T. Washington, clubwomen like Mary Church Terrell, activists like Ida B. Wells, or intellectuals like W.E.B. Du Bois, Madam Walker's heavily marketed rags-to-riches story doesn't seem like it belongs solely to the past or can be confined to her own historical context. The full history of the woman behind the name and image remains elusive, but this is precisely what it means to be an icon, especially an African American icon: a figure whose name and image move fans and inspire a host of meanings across the decades.

Madam C. J. Walker: The Making of an American Icon tells this story.

~

Acknowledgments

This book was shaped by numerous conversations with friends and colleagues on campus, at conferences, at the Huntington Library, and most recently, over Zoom. Thank you to Courtney Baker, Carol Berkin, Mijin Cha, Ross Lerner, Ainsley LeSure, Delia Mellis, Chandra Prescod-Weinstein, Tatiana Seijas, Terri Snyder, and Peter Vellon for offering encouragement, keeping me accountable, and helping me to think through various aspects of this project. Conference chats with Tyrone Freeman and A'Lelia Bundles were illuminating and very much appreciated. I am especially grateful to Kellie Carter Jackson, Sharla Fett, Tyler D. Parry, and Justin Gomer for reading chapters as the project developed. A special shout out goes to Kathleen Feeley who not only helped me better understand early twentieth-century celebrity culture, but also read and commented on the entire manuscript. Thank you to the Rowman & Littlefield team, especially John David Smith, Jon Sisk, Benjamin Knepp, and Elaine McGarraugh, all of whom exhibited extraordinary patience with me as I ever so slowly moved this manuscript to completion.

Thank you to Doug Remley at the Smithsonian National Museum of African American History and Culture, and the staff at the Indiana Historical Society and the Denver Public Library. Funding from the Occidental College Faculty Enrichment Grant program and California State University, Fullerton's General Faculty Research Fund providing funds that helped to complete the project.

Thank you to the Norton, Doronio, and Ball families. Special thanks to my sister, Stephanie Ball and her husband Tom Sitzler for shepherding me around St. Louis and Denver and always sharing their good cheer and optimism. It's been fourteen years now, and Abby continues to nap next to me as I tap away on my laptop. She is a good dog. Brian Michael Norton remains my very best editor, best friend, and best everything. Always.

My parents, Gene and Carolyn Ball, have given me more than I can ever say. Mom and Dad: this book is for you.

CHAPTER ONE

~

Daughter

Nothing about Madam C. J. Walker's origins—or, for that matter, the first three decades of her life—suggested that she would somehow fashion herself into a successful businesswoman, a philanthropist, and ultimately, an American icon. By the time of her death at the age of fifty-one on May 25, 1919, the woman who had renamed herself Madam C. J. Walker was famous for the financial success of her Madam C. J. Walker Manufacturing Company and her popular hair-care products for women of African descent. By then she had become a celebrity to black Americans across the country, while her image—immortalized in the photograph she used in the advertisements and packaging for her products—was instantly recognizable to millions of black consumers both within and outside the United States. In interviews, promotional stories, and profiles in newspapers across the country, black and white journalists offered details about Madam Walker's captivating stage presence, her fashion sense, her stylish automobiles and homes, her efforts to improve the economic and political status of people of African descent around the world, and, of course, her personal wealth. With a total estate valued at somewhere between one half and one million dollars to at the time of her death, Madam Walker had—according to the official press release issued by her Madam C. J. Walker Manufacturing Company—secured the title of "the richest colored woman in the world, and the greatest colored philanthropist." Thus, by 1919, Madam Walker had fully and completely transformed herself from "Sarah Breedlove," the rather ordinary girl she had been in her youth, into the extraordinary "Madam C. J. Walker," a figure who embodied all the hopes and aspirations of the modern African American woman at the start of the twentieth century.

But that is where her remarkable life ends.

Madam C. J. Walker's story actually began quite differently, in a small one-room cabin on a cotton plantation in northeastern Louisiana in the aftermath of the Civil War. Born on December 23, 1867, and given the name Sarah by her parents, she was the fifth child of Minerva and Owen Breedlove, former slaves who now lived and worked as tenant farmers on the estate of their former owner. Her family was, by all accounts, quite poor, and her parents could neither read nor write. And as was the case with the vast majority of African Americans born during slavery or in the turbulent years immediately after emancipation, the details of Sarah Breedlove's family history and earliest years remain shrouded in mystery. Still, in sketching out the broadest outlines of her origins, we can get a good sense of the profound chasm between the young girl she once was and the cultural icon she would later become. We can also gain an understanding of the social and cultural context that would guide her later in her life as she transformed herself into the epitome of the modern black American woman.

There is no record of where Sarah's parents were born, or how they first met, or even when they first decided to pledge their lives to each other and start a family. As enslaved men and women, Owen and Minerva were legally classified as property rather than citizens, and without the ability to read or write they were unable to leave behind a record of their personal opinions or life experiences. But it is clear that by 1848, when they were both about nineteen years old, Minerva and Owen were listed as two of the nine slaves owned by Robert Burney, a young aspiring planter just establishing his foothold in Delta, Louisiana, and entering into a business partnership with a Mississippi entrepreneur named Oliver O. Woodman. Financial documents assessed Owen's value at $700. Minerva was valued at $600.

At the time, Delta was a small settlement of cotton farms and plantations scattered along the Louisiana side of the Mississippi River. Situated on the border of Madison Parish in the far-flung, northeastern corner of the state, Delta and its surrounding environs had none of the bustle and activity of the state's famous port city of New Orleans, located roughly two hundred miles further down the river. Rather, Delta's closest cities and towns were actually across the state line in Mississippi: The river port of Vicksburg lay directly across the Mississippi River, just five miles away, while the state capital, Jackson, stood roughly fifty miles east. The village of Delta, Louisiana, meanwhile, remained a remote, rural outpost that was fairly typical of the Mississippi delta, a region that stretched northward into the state of Mississippi on the other side of the river. It was in this section of the country where a small number of slave owners like Robert Burney reaped the financial benefits of a rapidly expanding agricultural economy built upon the physical and repro-ductive labor of enslaved black men and women like Owen and Minerva Breedlove.

In the earliest decades of the nineteenth century, this part of the country was considered the young nation's Southwest, a relatively wild and sparsely settled frontier when compared with the long-established states of the eastern seaboard. But a series of dramatic technological, demographic, and political developments rapidly transformed the region. After the Louisiana Purchase in 1803, a growing number of white migrants and planters from the East began carving out new farms and plantations not only in the newly acquired territory, but also along the various Alabama, Mississippi, and northern Florida waterways that fed into the mighty Mississippi and flowed to the major international port city of New Orleans. The popularization of the innovative paddle wheel steamboat suddenly freed ships from their cen-turies-old dependence on the sail, making it possible for flat-bottomed cargo vessels to transport people, raw materials, and manufactured products up and down waterways at a relatively quick pace. Meanwhile, with the advent of Eli Whitney's cotton gin, patented in 1793, field laborers could now remove the seeds from bolls of cotton with less difficulty and greater speed. This made the cultivation of the hearty, short staple variety of cotton a viable possibil-ity and potentially lucrative avenue for those who sought to gain wealth by growing agricultural products for national and international markets. With the knowledge that the cotton plant flourished in this part of the country, aspiring planters like Burney soon began buying property in Alabama, Mis-sissippi, and Louisiana, as well as the Florida panhandle, explicitly for the purpose of raising this profitable crop. And they migrated to the region in growing numbers, transporting their enslaved labor force—people like Mi-nerva and Owen—with them.

This demographic shift increased in speed and intensity in the years after 1830. With investors, land speculators, bankers, farmers, and aspiring plant-ers competing to purchase and profit off this expanding "Empire of Cotton," President Andrew Jackson embarked on what the federal government of-ficially called an Indian removal policy—in fact a genocidal campaign to drive the Deep South's indigenous population out of the Old Southwest. Over the next two years, federal troops forced virtually all of the members of the Creek, Choctaw, and Chickasaw nations, along with the Seminole and Cherokee further east, off of their lands in the southeastern United States.

Driven along a route the Cherokee named the Trail of Tears, the members of these nations were compelled to rebuild their lives in the newly created territory of Oklahoma. Their expulsion by the US government left vast swaths of fertile land available for eager white investors and aspiring planters, men like Burney who moved to the region in hopes of making a fortune. White newcomers to the region sought to purchase enslaved laborers, a demand that fueled the expansion of the interstate, or domestic slave trade. This market in human property had supplanted the Atlantic slave trade after 1808, when the federal ban on the importation of slaves from Africa went into effect. Now, with an insatiable need for laborers to work their new lands, cotton and sugar planters in states like Louisiana, Mississippi, and Alabama turned to slave owners in Upper South states like Kentucky, Maryland, North Carolina, and Virginia. These Upper South planters, in the midst of their own agricultural shift from tobacco cultivation to less labor-intensive cereals and grains, took advantage of the opportunity to profit off of the bodies they no longer needed to till their fields. And over the next four decades, they steadily supplied Southern buyers with African-descended bondswomen and men like Owen and Minerva, selling one million women, men, and children to slave dealers who separated them from their families and communities and shipped them southward for sale in the "Cotton Kingdom." Scholars estimate that as part of this trade, an additional one million enslaved people were sold in local, interstate, and regional markets along the way. Indeed, this forced migration remains the largest domestic migration in American history. Not surprisingly, this migration changed the economics and demographics of the Deep South dramatically. In states like Louisiana and Mississippi, the enslaved population expanded rapidly. According to historian Walter Johnson, "The census of 1820 recorded 69,064 slaves in Louisiana and 32,814 in Mississippi. Twenty years later, the respective numbers were 168,452 and 195,211. And twenty years after that, there were 331,726 slaves in Louisiana and 436,631 in Mississippi."

Consequently, by the time Owen and Minerva found themselves in Delta, this vast region had become both the heart of the nation's slave economy and the center of a global cotton economy. Often called the "black belt"—both for its rich soil and its high population of slaves—the Mississippi River valley soon emerged as the central artery for a national economic system built on the domestic slave trade; the cultivation, distribution, and exportation of cotton crops; and land speculation. By 1859, Mississippi and Louisiana had produced 864 million pounds of cotton for national and international markets. And by 1860, there were more millionaires per capita in the Mississippi valley than anywhere else in the United States. With the American boom and bust economy enabling men to gain (and lose) great wealth relatively quickly, the Mississippi delta and river valley in particular proved especially attractive to those white men and women who were eager to invest in human property and willing to take financial risks.

Robert Burney was clearly one such man. In his twenties and relatively new to the area, Burney intended to work his way up the economic ladder. First, he capitalized on the devastating losses generated by the financial panic of 1837 and purchased a tract of land in Delta, on the Louisiana side of the Mississippi River. He then made a good personal match in 1846, marrying a young woman named Mary Fredonia, a member of a prominent Mississippi slaveholding family. He further improved his future prospects in 1848, expanding his reach by staking out a claim on the Mississippi side of the river as well, and forming his cotton-farming and slave-speculating partnership with Oliver O. Woodman in 1848. Some of the enslaved people Burney and Woodman purchased joined the bondsmen and women already present in the area, and spent their days clearing the timber from Burney and Woodman's various properties and preparing the land for cotton cultivation. Both Minverva and Owen may have taken part in this arduous enterprise.

Burney must have been a clever speculator and effective taskmaster as well as an ambitious man, for by 1860, Burney had become an established planter in Delta, the proprietor of a thousand-acre plantation he called Grand View, overlooking the Mississippi River. In the intervening years, Burney also acquired sixty slaves, a sum of human property that ushered him into the ranks of the top 10 percent of slaveholders in the US South.

If Robert Burney thought of himself in the same ways that other slaveholding planters often imagined themselves on the eve of the Civil War, he probably preferred not to think of himself as a peddler of human flesh, but rather as a benevolent patriarch, an aristocratic gentleman who not only provided and cared for his wife and their six daughters, but also tended to the needs of all the enslaved men, women, and children who lived and worked on his expansive estate. He may even have believed that people of African descent like Minerva and Owen were far happier under his mastery and control than they would have been living their lives as free and independent men and women. Burney may even have had occasional personal misgivings about the institution of slavery. But he certainly never lost sight of the fact that the men and women he owned were the key to his current income and his future prosperity, capital investments that generated his and his children's wealth by producing his crops and giving birth to more bondservants, human beings with monetary value who he could work and transform into cash whenever necessary. Human though they were, Owen and Minerva remained fungible beings; no matter what mental gymnastics Burney might perform to mask his power over them, Minerva and Owen remained valuable *chattels personal*—tangible, movable property for men like Burney. Enslaved people like Minerva and Owen were not only the key to Burney's wealth and his family's future, they were the basis for his status as a successful Southern white planter and patriarch, the linchpin of his very identity and world.

Legally classified as chattel property—that is, movable personal belongings (as opposed to real estate) that could be bought, sold, or leased—Minerva and Owen Breedlove undoubtedly had less fondness for the institution of slavery than did their prosperous owner Robert Burney. For African Americans like the Breedloves, the experience of enslavement did not mean moving up the economic ladder or gaining social status in the community. Rather, enslavement meant engaging in arduous physical toil without compensation, with all of one's labors—including one's reproductive capacity—placed in the service of one's owner. Enslavement meant living with the threat of severe corporal punishment whenever a master, mistress, overseer, or random white person might choose to impose it. Indeed, the "black belt" region where the Breedloves lived in bondage garnered notoriety for the severity and violence of its labor regimen. The rapidly expanding cotton economy of the Mississippi River valley relied upon an increasingly brutal system of slavery, one where planters and overseers incorporated imaginative forms of punishment and coercion into the labor regimen in an effort to increase productivity—a 600 percent increase between 1820 and 1860—and compelled enslaved men and women to work virtually nonstop from sunup to sundown in the pursuit of one end: cotton.

Owen and Minerva's responsibilities at Grand View, however, are unclear. It is statistically most likely that both Owen and Minerva spent the bulk of their time cultivating cotton, as did the vast majority of the slaves in Louisiana and Mississippi. Indeed, with the high profitability of the crop, the region's planters were often inclined to forgo specialization of labor, putting as many of their bondsmen and women to work in the field as possible, including those who had been skilled laborers on their previous plantations in the Upper South. However, at some point later in her life, as she carefully crafted her public persona, Madam C. J. Walker would say that her father had been a blacksmith. Many biographers have followed suit, describing him as such. If this was indeed the case, then Owen may have had some authority among the enslaved population in the area. It is also possible that Minerva worked within the household of the plantation, carrying out domestic tasks for the Burney family. If so, Minerva would have been able to pass valuable information learned in the Burney household on to those laboring in the fields.

Whatever the case, whatever small degree of skill or privilege Minerva and Owen might have held in no way mitigated their status as slaves. Historians have demonstrated that being enslaved meant existing as a captive, one with virtually no legal protections and absolutely no right to self-determination. Scholars have also shown that the specter of violence haunted every member of every slave community, irrespective of their role in the labor force. Mistresses regularly asserted their authority within the household with mental and physical cruelty. And masters, drivers, and overseers ruthlessly extracted labor from those in the fields, driving slaves up and down the long rows at as rapid a pace as possible, weighing their sacks of cotton at the end of each day of harvest and whipping those who failed to meet or exceed the previous day's haul. Planters did not consider this to be cruel; this was standard practice for slaveholding in the region, a form of "management" advocated by the region's various authorities on slave care and plantation productivity.

Life as a slave also meant coexisting with the knowledge that oneself or one's children could be sold for any reason at any given moment, separated from friends, family, and kin forever. Given Delta's proximity to the Mississippi River and the port city of Vicksburg (not to mention their own fairly recent experiences of being bought and sold), the Breedloves surely remained sensitive to this threat of separation. Situated as they were—with the winding Mississippi River bounding the north, east and west sides of the Burney Grand View plantation, the Breedloves would have had an acute awareness of what it meant when a master decided to "put his slave in his pocket," or, in other words, sell a bondsman or bondswoman. From time to time, the Breedloves may even have seen, heard, or smelled the coffles of slaves being transported by steamboat down from Vicksburg on to the bustling cotton port of Natchez, Mississippi, all en route to their final destination: the famous slave trading pens and markets of New Orleans. But even if they somehow managed to avoid such scenes, they could not have remained unaware of the terrifying fact that sale remained an ever-present possibility for Owen and Minerva as well as their future progeny.

Still, like millions of others in their condition, Owen and Minerva Breedlove carved out lives for themselves, creating a family and a community in the midst of extremely oppressive circumstances. The enslaved men and women of the Mississippi River valley and its surrounding environs created a distinctive black Southern culture, one with a vibrant set of religious practices, expressive forms, and family traditions, stolen pleasures and secret amusements, as well as rituals of courtship and self-care in the midst of extreme violence, subjugation, and constant, inescapable toil. These black women and men like Minerva and Owen Breedlove built new kinship ties and forged new communities in Mississippi and Louisiana. And they established traditions and practices that continued to sustain their families through decades of uncertainty.

Indeed, the Breedloves' world and the future prospects of their children changed dramatically in 1861. Convinced that the US Constitution allowed them to enslave and own African Americans in perpetuity, many white Southerners feared that the election of a president with even the slightest opposition to the westward expansion of the peculiar institution posed a dire threat to the culture of the South and the system of racial slavery upon which it was based. So, almost immediately after Abraham Lincoln's election to the presidency in 1860, Southern states began seceding from the Union to form the Confederate States of America, an independent nation that purposefully protected slavery in its new constitution. In response to a Confederate attack on the federal arsenal at Fort Sumter on April 12, 1861, President Lincoln issued a call for northern states to provide soldiers to put down the Southern rebellion and preserve the United States. The subsequent Civil War raged on until April 1865.

For enslaved African Americans like the Breedloves, the Civil War immediately offered the promise of freedom from slavery. For although proslavery advocates insisted that people of African descent were happiest when enslaved, bondsmen and women yearned for freedom above all. For example, when Solomon Northup—a free black New Yorker who spent twelve years captive and enslaved in Louisiana after being kidnapped and sold into slavery during a trip to Washington, DC—published a memoir about his ordeal, he made a point of saying that "ninety-nine out of every hundred" bondsmen and women he met during his time in Louisiana "are intelligent enough to understand their situation, and to cherish in their bosoms the love of freedom, as passionately as themselves." So even in the earliest days of the war, enslaved men and women interpreted the American Civil War as an opportunity to claim their freedom. And whenever Union forces neared, they fled in droves from the farms and plantations of their owners to seek refuge behind the Union lines. Current estimates put the numbers of these wartime fugitives at approximately half a million. Defined as "contraband of war" in the earliest years of the conflict, many of these men and women performed labor in Union camps. The number of slaves escaping to Union lines increased after President Lincoln's 1863 Emancipation Proclamation liberated those enslaved in Confederate territory and thus officially transformed the Civil War from an effort to save the Union into a war to abolish slavery. And after 1863, many of these formerly enslaved black men enlisted in the Union Army's newly formed US Colored Troops, transforming their desire for freedom into active warfare against those who had once held them in bondage, and doing their part to liberate those wives, children, parents, and siblings they had left behind.

Approaching Union forces meant something quite different for the slave owner Robert Burney and his family, of course. And when the Union troops captured the port city of New Orleans in the spring of 1862 and began to press northward as part of their campaign against the city of Vicksburg, the Burneys found themselves directly in harm's way. Vicksburg stood just across the river and five miles north of Delta, and it seemed that Union forces would pass right through Delta as they prepared to lay siege to the vital port city. So, much like many Southern slaveholders who found themselves in the path of advancing Union troops, the Burneys hastily gathered their possessions and fled to what they hoped would be safer ground. Taking the Breedloves with them, the Burneys crossed the Mississippi River and took shelter in a rented home in Morton, Mississippi. At the time, Minvera and Owen had three young children under the age of eight: a daughter named Louvenia, born sometime around 1854, and two sons named Alexander and James, born around 1858 and 1861, respectively.

The Breedloves remained with the Burneys for the duration of the war and traveled back to Delta with them soon after the Confederate surrender in the spring of 1865. When they all finally returned to the plantation by the river, they found that Grand View, like so many spaces transformed by the war, had changed a great deal. While they were away, Union troops commandeered Grand View, using it as a base camp for more than three thousand Union soldiers and escaping slaves, or "contraband," who they put to work on an ill-fated attempt to construct a canal to aid in the siege of Vicksburg. Illness abounded in contraband camps such as these, generating a high mortality rate for African Americans. Indeed, the remains of hundreds of those men and women now lay in mass graves around the Burney property. Meanwhile, the main home and the outbuildings of Grand View had been destroyed. In the place of these structures, the property now contained the physical evidence of the Union Army's failed canal project and a freedmen's camp, one of many dreary sites spread across the postwar South where displaced bondsmen and women crowded together in poor conditions in the aftermath of the war. Although the Thirteenth Amendment to the Constitution outlawing slavery would not be ratified by the states and adopted by the nation until December that year, for all intents and purposes, these bondsmen men and women were now free.

Like them, the Breedloves too were freedpeople, with the right to pack up their young family and leave the Burneys behind. Ultimately, however, the Breedloves remained at Grand View. And in the months that followed, as the Burneys reestablished control over their land and estate, the members of the two families had to negotiate a new kind of working relationship and establish a new set of rules for interacting with each other. No longer master and slave, as they had been for decades, the Burneys and the Breedloves now had to learn how to live and work together as employee and employer, or landowner and tenant—each with a new set of responsibilities and obligations. For many former slaves and masters, this adjustment remained difficult and unresolved. Former bondsmen and women like the Breedloves usually wanted to fully experience freedom, and, according to their definitions of the term, construct their lives in ways that did not reproduce the exploitative power dynamics of slavery. Freedmen and women like the Breedloves sought clear labor contracts and insisted that they be fairly compensated for their work. They also wanted to live without the constant oversight, coercion, and violence that defined their daily toil under slavery, and to acquire autonomy and independence for themselves and their families. Toward these ends, they insisted—often over the objections of their employers—on organizing themselves into family units rather than in the large gangs that had characterized field work under the system of slavery in the cotton kingdom. And they prioritized attention to the domestic needs of their own families, rather than placing the needs of their employers before their own.

The Burneys, meanwhile, probably hoped to keep as many of their old hands on the land as possible, even if it meant taking the unprecedented step of paying their former slaves for their labor. Perhaps the Burneys reasoned that having field and domestic workers with knowledge about the needs of the local soil and the seasonal flooding patterns of the river would make the process of rebuilding Grand View that much easier. The Burneys surely hoped to begin the process of restoring their home to its previous condition and begin planting cotton for the next season. Still, for the Burneys, emancipation must have come as a terrible shock. If they were no longer masters who purchased, owned, and profited from the labor and reproductive labor of human beings, then what were they? Unfortunately for the Burneys, they had very little time to fully acclimate themselves to their new and diminished roles as employers. Both Mary Fredonia and Robert Burney died within months of each other in 1866: Robert died of a stroke and Mary succumbed to cholera soon after.

Despite the deaths of their former owners, Minerva and Owen Breedlove, now with four young children in their household thanks to the recent arrival of Owen Jr., decided to remain on the Burney family property in Delta and rent from Burney's heirs. This was not unusual. Although many freedmen and women relocated in search of favorable employment after the Civil War, most settled near or within the immediate vicinity of where they had most recently been living. This particular decision made sense for the Breedloves for several reasons. Owen and Minerva had lived in Delta for at least twenty years, and they were already close to forty years old. Deeply familiar with Delta and the surrounding communities in Madison Parish, the Breedloves had, together with their neighbors, created a community. Staying on the Burney estate allowed them to preserve some sense of stability in an un-certain world and maintain a connection with their past. Moreover, Owen and Minerva had their children with them. Unlike countless freedmen and women, the family unit Minerva and Owen built together over the years ap-pears not to have been disrupted either by sale or by the war. Consequently, they didn't need to travel, like so many other African Americans did at the time, in an effort to relocate far-flung family members. Finally, Owen and Minerva Breedlove already knew the Burney property intimately. For more than a decade they had been expected to read the needs of the land and the temperament of the Mississippi River bounding it, and they had learned to order their lives around the rhythms of the annual cycle of planting, tend-ing, and harvesting at Grand View. With such deep knowledge of the region, they probably hoped to have a shot at making a good economic start as a free family. Sharecropping or tenant farming was not exactly ideal, but it did, initially at least, feel somewhat more independent than slavery.

Staying on familiar ground may have also made it easier to navigate an unfamiliar and dangerous political terrain. Although racial chattel slavery had now been abolished, Southern whites of all classes did not easily relin-quish their legal rights and social privileges to define the terms of black labor and hold power over black bodies. Indeed, former slaves and their children found that their newfound freedom was contested at every turn. Even Freed-men's Bureau officials, representatives of the federal government ostensibly charged with the responsibility of protecting the rights of black Southerners, pressured freedmen and women into labor contracts with their former own-ers. Southern planters, meanwhile, often failed to uphold the terms of these contracts. Accustomed to wielding authority over every aspect of black life, former masters and mistresses and other Confederates interpreted any expres-sion of African American freedom—whether it be freedom of movement or assembly, the use of married names and titles, requests to be paid wages for their labor, or attempts to vote—as a direct challenge and a threat to white supremacy, characterizing it all as part of a continuum of profoundly unsettling behavior; to them, these were dangerous attitudes and actions indicative of black people's insolence and ingratitude, forms of behavior that needed to be dealt with great haste. The Black Codes enacted by Mississippi in 1865, indenturing black children and criminalizing, among other things, the movement and free assembly of black Americans, arose in in response to these concerns and quickly adopted by other Southern states. So too did vigilante violence against African Americans, often perpetrated by the newly created Ku Klux Klan. Although these Black Codes would soon be repealed, the status and place of former slaves like the Breedloves and their children continued to be contested over the next decade during a period known as the Reconstruction era.

In 1866, Republicans, many of whom found common cause with abolitionists before the Civil War, took control of Congress and pushed through a series of acts, policies, and constitutional amendments designed to protect freedmen and women from their former owners and others who sought to restore a version of the old slave regime. Passing the Fourteenth and Fifteenth Amendments to the Constitution in 1866 and 1868, Congress now moved to extend the rights of citizenship to all those born or naturalized in the United States—including those of African descent—and expanded the right to vote to all male citizens. By 1875, a federal Civil Rights Act made access to public space a right for all Americans, irrespective of race. Each of these developments was met with fierce resistance on the part of white Southerners, who interpreted the extension of civil and political rights to people of African descent as "Negro rule." Black Southerners would experience the violent repercussions of this resistance to change throughout the entire period of Reconstruction and beyond. This would be the beginning of a long and protracted battle over the meaning of freedom for people of African descent in the United States.

So by 1867, with their old master and mistress dead, Owen and Minerva were living on the property of their former owner, eking out a living as sharecroppers or tenant farmers, and trying—like so many African Americans in the years after emancipation—to save up enough money to someday purchase their own land and become independent masters of their own small worlds. As renters working a plot of land on the Burney property, the Breedloves probably handed over between 30 and 50 percent of the cotton crop they harvested to the landowner at the end of the season. At this time, they also paid for the year's food and supplies purchased on credit from the local store. What remained after these transactions, they could keep for themselves. When the harvest was good, the Breedloves might have come out ahead, earning money to put toward the expenses of the coming year. But when the cotton harvest was poor, as it was in 1866 and 1867, they needed to borrow against the upcoming year's crop to order the seed, tools, and food and clothing necessary for them to try their luck again. Unsurprisingly, then, many Southern tenant farmers and sharecroppers soon found themselves locked in a cycle of debt and poverty that lasted well into the twentieth century.

Into this uncertain new world, Minerva and Owen Breedlove's daughter Sarah was born in December 1867. And although she would later achieve the kind of wealth and celebrity status that few American women—let alone black American women—could ever even imagine, Sarah Breedlove lived the first years of her life in circumstances that were fairly typical of those experienced by the vast majority of African American girls in the second half of the nineteenth century. Like most sharecroppers and tenant farmers, Sarah's family had little in the way of creature comforts. The family lived in a typical one-room cabin without indoor plumbing and with very little in the way of furnishings or luxuries. These dwellings usually contained a single, large open-hearth fireplace used for cooking meals. This also served as the cabin's only source of warmth during the winter months. To understand the simplicity of these cabins, it is helpful to hear how Solomon Northup described the Louisiana cabin that served as his shelter during the twelve years he spent in Bayou Boeuf, Louisiana. Northup recalled that his cabin was "constructed of logs, without floor or window." Although the cracks between the logs admitted "sufficient light" during the day, in "stormy weather the rain drives through them, rendering it comfortless and extremely disagreeable." By 1869, Sarah Breedlove shared her family's cabin with her mother and father, four older siblings, and one younger brother named Solomon.

Like other African American girls growing up in such close quarters, Sarah likely spent a great deal of time under the watchful eyes of her parents and older siblings. And from them, Sarah Breedlove had the opportunity to learn a number of lessons. With no public school available for the black children of Delta (the Louisiana state legislature having refused to fund schools for the black children of Louisiana in 1874), the bulk of Sarah Breedlove's early childhood education probably revolved around the folk customs that shaped African American rural culture. The region remained rich with older African and homegrown black American folk traditions well into the twentieth century. As a child growing up in this context, Sarah Breedlove might have heard stories and folk tales about Africa, or stories about flying Africans. She would have learned about tricksters like Brer Rabbit who outwitted the more powerful Brer Fox. And she would have known about or perhaps even witnessed women healers and conjurers use folk remedies to care for those in their communities who neither trusted nor could afford white medical doctors. These customs would have imbued her with respect for the traditions of the past, strengthened the connection between Sarah and the other members of her rural black community, and shaped her future work as a beauty culturist, entrepreneur, and race woman.

From her mother and her older sister Louvenia, Sarah most certainly learned a number of beauty rituals, including how to care for and arrange her hair. As it was before emancipation, hair care remained a meaningful communal ritual for African American women and girls like Sarah. Evenings when enslaved women gathered together to style themselves in preparation for secret religious gatherings or festive community celebrations provided opportunities to socialize, support each other, and take pleasure in their own beauty. These moments contrasted starkly with their daily work regimen; the slave regime demanded that all forms of enslaved women's labor, including the ability to dress hair and style clothing, be placed in the service of their owners. After emancipation, black women's personal beauty rituals became politically contested terrain, with black women and girls eagerly embracing the opportunity to style themselves as they saw fit and white women who were no longer slave owners interpreting black women's style choices as a political affront. But during these moments, in their own private spaces, black women and girls turned their time, attention, and skills toward care of themselves and each other. In doing so, they continued a tradition that had long served as important emotional sustenance within slave communities across the Americas.

As a young girl, Sarah would have been expected to wait patiently each week while her older female kin combed the tangles out of her fragile, tightly coiled hair, separating it into small, neat sections before braiding each portion or wrapping each section of hair with long strands of cotton string, referred to as African threading by those who practice it in early twenty-first-century United States. The string served the utilitarian function of keeping tightly curled hair from getting tangled, but it also served as a styling tool that stretched out kinks and set ringlets or created waves. While Sarah would likely be sent outdoors with her hair tied up with string and uncovered, her mother and older sister Louvenia probably covered their own hair with a brightly colored cotton bandana or cloth after engaging in the same process or twisting or braiding their hair. The bandana kept their hair protected from dust and dirt as Minerva and Louvenia engaged in the hard work of maintaining the household and helping with seasonal field labor. But the headwrap served more than a utilitarian function. From at least the eighteenth century, African-descended women in the Americas chose brightly colored and patterned cloth whenever they could, placing these headwraps in the service of their own particular style. In keeping with this tradition, the Breedlove women may have also styled their bandanas and headwraps, arranging them with care and tying them into intricate knots. On the weekends, the women and girls would help each other unwrap their hair and arrange it for Sunday school, church services, or special community events.

These community gatherings would have been especially important to the Breedlove family. Institutions like African American churches, which had largely been confined to clandestine activity before emancipation, now came out into the open as formal organizations, making it possible for their members to worship freely in the light of day. Church services offered respite from a long week of toil and brought people scattered across the countryside together in fellowship. In addition to providing weekly religious services, African American churches also assisted the members of their congregation in a number of other ways. Members often banded together to create dues-collecting mutual aid societies that members drew upon for support during moments of financial hardship. Meanwhile, Sunday schools often provided rudimentary education for adults as well as children. Additionally, African American churches emerged as a fertile training ground for the generation of African American leaders who went on to become active in state and local politics during the Reconstruction era. In fact, in 1867, the year Sarah was born, the Breedloves' family minister, Curtis Pollard, served as a delegate elected to the Louisiana State Constitutional Convention of 1867. Pollard later became a Republican state senator for Louisiana.

As the daughter of parents who worked land owned by others, Sarah probably did not expect her own father to run for office. But she surely grew to understand that hard work was a daily fact of life for black women and men alike. Children as young as Sarah often helped their older siblings and parents chop or pick cotton when it was time to harvest the fields. Indeed, well into the twentieth century, many school districts across the South scheduled black school terms around agricultural seasons. And black girls as young as ten years old might be sent to work as domestic laborers in white households to earn extra income for the family.

Although every member of a sharecropping or tenant farming family usually helped out in the fields whenever necessary, the Breedloves most likely maintained a gender division of labor within the home. Although African Americans had adhered to a gendered system of domestic labor before emancipation, now that they were free, former slaves considered the opportunity to place women's domestic work in the service of their own family and household without white interference to be emblematic of their new life as freed people. Certain responsibilities, such as cooking, childcare, and care for the sick and elderly, remained primarily the purview of wives and mothers, who would teach these skills to their daughters. These gendered skills continued to be transmitted from mother to daughter after emancipation, and Sarah likely watched her older sister and her mother at these tasks. She may even have assisted with the household labor by caring for her new baby brother while her mother and sister engaged in more onerous tasks. She would have watched her mother and Louvenia cook every day in the open-hearth fireplace and perhaps helped them as they swept out the dirt and dust, part of the constant battle to keep the rough one-room cabin as habitable as possible. She would have learned how the women in the household spun any excess cotton into thread and later wove that thread into rough homespun fabric. She would have observed them toiling over the family laundry every week. By the age of six, she most certainly would have aided them in these endeavors, either by helping out with small tasks or by minding her younger brother or tending the family garden patch. With Minerva and her daughters managing the household while Owen their sons daily engaged in the work of planting, cultivating and chopping cotton, the entire Breedlove family made an effort to ensure that their household economy was as productive as possible.

As this system of household production suggests, newly freed families like the Breedloves emphasized the importance of maintaining strong familial bonds. And to underscore their commitment to each other and their children, Owen and Minerva formally married in November 1869, in a ceremony conducted by Reverend Pollard. Unable to legally marry while enslaved and always subject to having their families sundered by sale, freedmen and women like the Breedloves often appreciated the opportunity to have their marriages legalized and sanctioned by the state. While some former slaves simply adhered to the vows they made before emancipation, others formalized their long-standing unions anew immediately after the war. After two good cotton-producing years in 1868 and 1869, it seems that the Breedloves finally secured enough extra money to pay the $100 fee—quite a considerable sum in the period—required for a marriage license. And, likely in the presence of two-year-old Sarah and her five brothers and sisters, Minerva and Owen legally wed, each signing their marriage certificate with an X.

This momentous family event symbolized how much had changed for the Breedlove family by 1869. No longer enslaved, they now sought to claim for themselves all the advantages that came with freedom. And although they had little in the way of social status or financial security to bequeath to their youngest daughter, Sarah, they could take solace in the fact that all of their children could at least have a future predicated on the expansive possibilities of freedom rather than the harsh realities of chattel slavery that had shaped so much of their own lives. At the same time, however, Minerva and Owen Breedlove must have known that their children continued to face a host of challenges. Life as a tenant farmer or sharecropper was not easy. Former Confederates and slave owners continued to push back against the possibility of black advancement. With every election cycle, the federal government seemed less concerned about white Southerners' violent efforts to suppress the votes of African Americans. And freedom alone did not offer any protection against the extreme poverty, illness, or high mortality rates that plagued black families and communities in Louisiana, Mississippi, and beyond. In fact, these circumstances soon took their toll on the Breedlove family. Sometime before 1874, Minerva Breedlove died and Owen remarried. His second marriage did not last long, however, for by 1877, Owen too had passed away.

At just ten years of age, Sarah now found herself in the position of countless black children at the end of the Reconstruction era: orphaned and at risk. With no parents, no social standing, and little in the way of educational or economic opportunity before her, young Sarah Breedlove—the daughter of slaves—made a decision that hundreds of thousands of African Americans in similar circumstances would make in the coming decades. She would leave Delta, Louisiana, behind and begin to move.

CHAPTER TWO

~

Migrant

In 1877, Sarah Breedlove and her siblings faced an uncertain future in the United States. In the waning years of the Reconstruction era, paramilitary groups known as White Leagues and White Liners terrorized black voters across the South, driving black Republican officeholders from their elected positions. That year, the federal government withdrew the last of the Union troops who, at least theoretically, served as a check on the antiblack violence dished out by white Southerners who never accepted the emancipation and freedom of black Americans. The elections that followed remained violent—sometimes morphing into full-blown purges in locations throughout the South—until the vast majority of Southern black male voters were driven from the polls and the last black elected officials and political appointees were removed from office. In 1883, the Supreme Court ruled that the 1875 Civil Rights Act's provision barring discrimination in public spaces (such as hotels, parks, restaurants, and forms of transportation) was unconstitutional. Soon afterward, Southern states began passing a wave of legislation, revising state constitutions, and building a de jure racial caste system that restricted black Americans' access to education and public space while keeping the overwhelming majority of African Americans subject to economic exploitation and political disfranchisement. Pieced together through an elaborate system of laws, customs, daily rituals of humiliation, and extreme forms of antiblack violence, this system, known colloquially as Jim Crow, subjugated African Americans and provided the architecture of the region's white supremacy. Meanwhile, the majority of black Southerners remained bound to the land for generations. Many of them quickly found themselves and their families trapped in a cycle of debt peonage, unable to leave the land they worked as sharecroppers, tenant farmers, or contract laborers. Thus, Sarah Breedlove found herself orphaned at the precise moment that the United States began a seventy-year-long backlash against former slaves and their descendants.

Of course, a young child like Sarah couldn't have predicted any of these developments in 1877. Instead, what she might have noticed was that various constituencies—former planters and former slaves, politicians, white and black men and women—negotiated and fought over the possibilities, limitations, and parameters of freedom for African Americans. She would also have seen that in the midst of the uncertainty of this period, black Americans persevered. Despite being subject to a range of constraints as well as astonishing acts of violence and political terrorism, black Americans like the Breedloves used all the means at their disposal to claim the fullest measure of liberty possible. They strove to become their best selves and live their best lives. Each individual black Southerner's ability to do so remained shaped by their gender, their access to education and economic opportunities, and the support of their family members and surrounding community. And even then, there were no guarantees.

In many respects, Sarah's experiences during these years of her life were, once again, unremarkable. Indeed, many years later, once she had shed her identity as Sarah Breedlove and successfully refashioned herself into the famous Madam C. J. Walker, she would describe her childhood and youth in three short phrases: "I was orphaned at seven, married at fourteen, a widow at twenty." In other words, she generally characterized her childhood and youth as difficult but worth little commentary, focusing instead on reiterating and disseminating the story of her rise from obscurity to phenomenal success. The details of her early years, it seems, she preferred to keep hidden away from the general public. Perhaps she used this shorthand knowing her audience would understand and identify with the basic contours of her life, recognize the extraordinary nature of her socioeconomic mobility and continue to identify with her as she expanded her beauty empire. Whatever the case, her persistent use of this shorthand and refusal to elaborate has made the task of uncovering information about the first four decades of her life exceedingly difficult for scholars.

What we do know about Sarah Breedlove's youth—the period in which she was "orphaned at seven, married at fourteen, a widow at twenty"—and her subsequent years as a young woman is that Sarah's earliest life experiences were far from uncommon for women of African descent in the decades after the Civil War. On one hand, her experiences show just how difficult it was for men and women of African descent to claim their freedom in the aftermath of slavery. At the same time, however, they demonstrate just how tenacious African Americans were in the pursuit of all of the fruits of liberty. During this period, the masses of black Southerners invariably sought to define the terms of their own labor, to remove themselves from constant white oversight, to take the necessary steps to protect themselves from violence, and to secure the safety of their families. When they were unable to do so, they voted with their feet and moved on to new towns and cities within and beyond the South. Ultimately, Sarah and her siblings would do the same, joining a growing stream of black Southern migrants who put down roots in new locales and crafted new lives for themselves in communities across the nation. In the process, Sarah acquired many of the skills she needed to facilitate her remarkable transformation from one of many black migrant women whose stories are largely lost to history into the celebrity known as Madam C. J. Walker.

As a young black orphan in 1877, Sarah Breedlove found herself in particularly vulnerable circumstances. There was very little in the way of a safety net for Southern black children in the 1870s and '80s, and unaccompanied black children continued to be susceptible to incarceration by authorities and forced to labor in white homes or on white-owned farms. Although a new generation of Southern black women would soon begin banding together and founding organizations that would help to care for the well-being of children like Sarah, the formal institutional infrastructure that these sorts of community organizations and orphanages would ultimately provide for black communities was still, for the most part, a decade away. The Freedmen's Bureau might have stepped in to help in its own way—it had for a time put unaccompanied black children up for adoption or out for hire as laborers—but the federal government disbanded the Freedmen's Bureau at the end of Reconstruction. And given its record of placing black children in exploitative circumstances with white landowners rather than with the African American aunts, uncles, and other relatives who hoped to claim their youngest and most vulnerable family members, it is unclear how helpful the bureau may have been. Consequently, rather than relying on formal institutions, children like Sarah relied heavily on their own families and extended kinship networks.

Kinship networks remained essential for the survival and health of black Southerners for generations. This tradition stemmed in part from the dislocations and losses caused by the antebellum domestic slave trade, when one million enslaved African Americans were sold from the Upper South to the Deep South. This extraordinary forced migration—the largest in US history—consistently broke up family units in states like Virginia, Kentucky, and Maryland; those left behind relied on each other to sustain what was left of their family units. Meanwhile, those African Americans who were up-rooted and sold to the Deep South embraced what scholars often call "fictive kin" to help them navigate their unfamiliar circumstances, create new families, and build communities in states like Mississippi, Alabama, Louisiana, and Texas. In doing so, these black Southerners extended and repurposed a practice that first began with the Atlantic slave trade, when those who were taken from their families in Africa and sold and transported to North America established new relationships with men, women, and children of African descent during their journey. Ultimately, as historian Tera K. Hunter puts it, these "broad understandings of kinship encouraged black women to assume responsibility for needy children other than their natural offspring." Thus, steeped in this long-standing tradition of kinship, young Sarah Breedlove now relied upon her older brothers and sisters for help and support.

By the time of their parents' deaths, the Breedlove children were choosing not to stay, as their parents had done, on the plantation in Delta, Louisiana. Instead, they, like many of the black residents of this sparsely populated Louisiana county, began leaving the area. One by one, the Breedlove children decided to exchange the familiar rural life for the possibility of greater opportunity in the nearby city of Vicksburg, Mississippi. Sarah's older brother Alexander was about twenty years old at the time and working as a porter in the city. Her brother Owen may have been in Vicksburg as well, although, still a child himself, he leaves less of an imprint in the historical record. Moreover, the oldest Breedlove sibling, Louvenia, now about twenty-four years of age, was either engaged or newly married to a man named Jesse Powell, who also resided in the city. So, early in the summer of 1878, Sarah and Louvenia took the short twenty-five-cent ferry ride across the river and headed to Vicksburg. The ten-year-old Sarah moved in with her older sister and her new husband.

While this move must certainly have felt like a momentous personal milestone for Sarah and Louvenia, the decision to relocate from the sparsely populated Delta, Louisiana, to Vicksburg, Mississippi—a city with a population that hovered around twelve thousand—made the Breedlove children participants in a larger regional demographic transformation. In 1870, only 10 percent of the Southern black population lived in towns with populations larger than twenty-five hundred residents (this was "urban" according to the census categories of that time). But in the years after the Civil War,

Southern cities like Vicksburg, Atlanta, Charleston, and Memphis began experiencing an influx of black arrivals. By the turn of the twentieth century, 20 percent of Southern African Americans resided in the region's towns and cities. When asked why they would make such a move, freedmen and women invariably replied that they moved to Southern towns and cities to experience freedom to the fullest, to escape the watchful eyes of their former owners, or to simply "enjoy their freedom" in a city or town where they could live their lives "much easier" than they had on the plantation. By choosing to make the move to Vicksburg in 1878, then, the Breedlove siblings were at the leading edge of what eventually became a large-scale rural-to-urban migration for black Southerners, a demographic shift that scholars such as historian Earl Lewis view as "an act of individual and collective empowerment," and an essential part of the African American struggle "to improve their place in the region's political economy and to share the nation's bounty as full citizens." To put it another way, the Breedlove siblings relocated in search of freedom.

In the most immediate terms, migrants like the Breedloves hoped to find freedom from violence. With strength in numbers, cities offered African Americans the possibility of a refuge from the antiblack violence they might have faced in sparsely populated rural areas like Delta. As the recently emancipated traveled to new locations, they often gravitated toward counties, towns, and neighborhoods with an established black presence. Given the prevalence of white hostility and antiblack violence, these rural-to-urban migrants sought safety, security, and something akin to freedom in numbers. Notably, young single women and widows with young children also migrated to larger towns and cities across the South in increasing numbers during the period. They hoped that cities and towns like Vicksburg would leave them less vulnerable to the forms of exploitation, domestic abuse, and sexual violence that endangered them in the isolated countryside. They also hoped to find work. A single mother who had difficulty supporting her family as a sharecropper or tenant farmer expected to find more employment opportunities in a Southern town or a city.

Cities like Vicksburg also contained more opportunities for sociability and community life than African Americans were likely to find in sparsely populated rural areas. Schools—however limited in scope—were much more likely to be found in towns and cities as well. Although they certainly existed on a smaller scale in the countryside, it was in towns and cities with a significant and concentrated black population that African American mutual aid societies, church auxiliaries, and benevolent associations thrived. These societies served a crucial set of functions for the poor and working-class men and women who sustained them, for mutual aid societies and benevolent associations provided dues-paying members with benefits should individuals lose a job or a loved one. These organizations also formed the basis for an expansive black associational culture that would soon flower across the nation. Institutions such as these, along with the sociability they provided, might have been especially appealing to the widows, young single women, and girls who moved to Southern towns and cities in search of employment. These were, as the historian Jacqueline Jones puts it, some of the "social consequences of freedom" for freedom's first generation.

Vicksburg, in particular, may have seemed like a good option to the Breedloves for several reasons. First, its proximity to Delta certainly must have made it an obvious choice. Second, its black population had tripled since the Civil War. This demographic shift began in 1863, midway through the Civil War, when Union troops occupied the city, making Vicksburg a destination for fugitive slaves fleeing to Union lines. During the Reconstruction era, African American men held political office in the city and the surrounding county, including the posts of sheriff and justice of the peace. The city also contained black churches and schools. All of this suggested that Vicksburg might be a city in which the Breedloves could put down new roots and build new lives for their families.

Most importantly for their long-term future prospects, migrants like the Breedloves hoped that Southern cities like Vicksburg, Mississippi, would provide the economic opportunity that rural areas like Delta, Louisiana, could not offer them. Like other black Southerners who moved from the farm to the city in the years after Reconstruction, they hoped to secure jobs with decent wages and carve out some measure of independence for themselves. Black men who had been skilled laborers or artisans under the former plantation regime often arrived in Southern cities with the expectation that their training and skills would land them similar positions in urban areas. However, they found it increasingly difficult to gain employment as artisans; in the post-Reconstruction era, white artisans often refused to work alongside skilled African American men. Instead black men found work building roads, canals, and railroads, and other forms of vital infrastructure for the emerging New South. Some sought work as waiters in restaurants or porters in hotels. Those African American men with some education might find employment as teachers in newly established black schools. And a few served the African American community as ministers or opened their own small business establishments.

Black women found their employment options to be even more limited than those of their male counterparts. For the select few black women who were fortunate enough to receive an education during the years immediately after emancipation, teaching in one of the new schools for black children offered a potential career path. A small minority with skills as milliners or dressmakers might also find work in larger Southern cities like Charleston, South Carolina. But for most rural black migrant women, these positions remained out of reach. Instead, black women tended to find employment as cooks, maids, children's caretakers, and laundresses—forms of domestic labor with overlapping sets of responsibilities. Even with these limited job prospects, migrant women often found Southern cities to be more appealing than rural areas where sharecropping and tenant farming dominated. In these locales, women without husbands, whether widowed or young and single, stood little chance of leasing or running a farm on their own. So rural black women migrated to Southern cities in increasing numbers over the second half of the nineteenth century. For these reasons, cities often had imbalanced sex ratios, with black women residents outnumbering their male counterparts. These women and girls, like Louvenia and Sarah, usually sought positions as domestic workers in white households.

Louvenia and Sarah arrived in Vicksburg with an especially limited set of employment options. Born on a plantation to parents who worked the land, neither Louvenia nor Sarah received the type of extensive training that would have made it possible to find positions as cooks in white households. Cooks spent years learning how to prepare meals by memorizing recipes, cooking in open hearths, and baking cakes and pastries in cast iron pots placed in the fire or the chimney. Such knowledge, passed down from older women, took years of on-the-job training. Sarah, just ten years old at the time of her arrival in Vicksburg, most certainly was too young to find such employment. Entering into service as a maid or a child's nurse was a more reasonable possibility for both of the sisters, but white families usually hired child nurses and maids based on recommendations from white friends or other black domestics. Given their status as newcomers to the city, neither Louvenia nor Sarah was likely to have the necessary references to give them access to these positions.

It should come as no surprise, then, that a young girl like Sarah Breedlove, raised on a plantation with the most limited of schooling, would enter the laundry trade. Indeed, both Louvenia and Sarah began working as laundresses soon after their arrival in Vicksburg. Taking in laundry offered its own set of possibilities and limitations for African American women. First, doing laundry required very little overhead or investment. One needed to purchase a heavy iron pot for boiling clothes, soap for cleaning, and an iron and some starch. And after having outfitted herself in this way, a woman would simply need to create a client base for herself.

Moreover, the opportunity to find employment as a laundress remained ever present. Most white Southerners—even those who fell far below the ranks of the middle class and could not afford to hire a cook or a maid—hired a washerwoman to launder the family's linens, bedding, and clothing every week. For this labor, laundresses generally earned an average monthly wage of somewhere between four and eight dollars, a sum that placed laundresses at the bottom of the pay scale for domestics. Those who earned more did so by increasing their client base. A laundress might, for example, go door-to-door offering her services. Alternately, while engaged in other business, she might keep her eyes open for white women in need of laundry service. Given the emerging Jim Crow racial caste system and white Southerners' frequent assertions that "good" servants were, with the abolition of slavery, now very difficult for them to find, white women sometimes approached random black women whose dress or apparel they found pleasing in the hopes of engaging their services and employing them in their homes. Encounters like these taught black girls and young women like Sarah and Louvenia that their bodies served as their own best advertisements for their skill at the laundry trade.

Having secured clients, a laundress's workweek generally followed the same schedule. On Monday she traveled from house to house, picking up bundles of laundry from white individuals and families. Early morning hours might be spent picking through the city's garbage to collect old rags and discarded cinders—kindling and fuel necessary for a fire. After drawing gallons of water and filling large cast iron pots, she boiled, scrubbed, soaked, and rinsed the various items. She then hung the clothes and bedding up to dry in the yard outside her home if she were lucky enough to have one. If a woman didn't have access to outdoor space or the weather did not permit drying outdoors, she simply hung the clothes up inside her home. By the middle of the week, the clothes had dried, and she turned to the laborious task of ironing. To do this, she sprinkled starch on each item of clothing. She warmed stones in the fireplace, using them as heating devices for the heavy iron. She then ironed all of the items, folding each one and placing it neatly in a basket or bundle, ready to return to each family on Saturday. Sunday she kept for herself and her own family. On Monday the cycle began anew.

This remained an arduous form of labor well into the twentieth century, when automatic washing and drying appliances became available and afford-

able for middle-class households. Until that time, black laundresses dominated the laundry trade throughout the South.

Given the nature of the work—both its intense and constant labor re-
quirements and its low pay—the laundry trade remained, in many respects,
the least desirable form of employment for Southern black women. At the
same time, however, working as a laundress did have its perks. The opportunity to have "clients" rather than "employers" and to engage in one's
labor either in one's own domestic space or in the company of other black
women offered the possibility for black laundresses to feel somewhat more
independent than the nursemaids, cooks, and maids-of-all-work who spent
their days working under constant oversight in white households. Moreover,
the communal nature of their work instilled a sense of group affinity and a
distinct sense of political consciousness among these women. Laundresses
took enormous pride in their work and they exerted as much control over
the terms of their labor as they could. And laundresses soon acquired a reputation as black women who maintained a fierce sense of pride in their labor
and who remained committed to sisterhood and community empowerment.
Moreover, in the wake of emancipation, laundresses helped to set the new
terms for black women's wage labor in the late nineteenth-century South,
refusing to work for those white families who insufficiently compensated
them for their labor, and quitting and finding new clients when they found
the demands of a particular white household to be unfavorable. Indeed, laundresses in Jackson, Mississippi, engaged in a collective labor action in June
1866, just one year after the conclusion of the Civil War and formal emancipation. Although the details of the strike and its results are lost to history,
the women submitted a formal petition to the mayor of Jackson, notifying
the city of their intent to raise and charge "a uniform rate" for their services.
In 1881, Atlanta's washerwomen organized a citywide strike in an effort to
secure higher wages. Relying heavily on local churches, the woman organized
an association and passed resolutions declaring their intention to stop work
en masse until they received a fair price for their labor.

Actions such as these suggest that black girls and women like Sarah and
Louvenia experienced far more than daily drudgery and hard physical labor
when they entered the laundry trade. They learned how—perhaps in the
most fundamental way—to style themselves as independent artisans, con-
tractors, or entrepreneurs and to advertise and market their business in the
public square. Moreover, by working in concert with other black women,
they learned about the power and significance of black women's community.
This wasn't traditional schooling by any means. But it did serve as an important educational experience and as political training for Sarah Breedlove.

Indeed, it undoubtedly provided an important foundation for her to build upon years later as she transformed herself into Madam C. J. Walker.

While she may have been able to exert some authority over the terms of her labor as a laundress in Vicksburg, it is unlikely that Sarah Breedlove experienced much autonomy in her domestic circumstances. After all, she was a young girl living in Louvenia and Jesse Powell's household, in what were very likely rough and close quarters. While she may have been able to keep some of her earnings for herself, she likely contributed much of the money she made as a laundress to the family income. And she would have been expected to defer to the authority of her sister and brother-in-law, who was, of course, the head of the household. Later in life, without offering any specific details about his personality or behavior or the nature of their family dynamic, Madam Walker would describe her brother-in-law as "cruel," characterizing his cruelty as the impetus for her decision to leave her sister Louvenia's care. Even under the very best of circumstances, it is not hard to imagine that a girl going through adolescence might feel somewhat stifled by domestic conditions such as these and anxious to carve out a more independent life or family unit on her own terms. As the historian Jacqueline Jones has noted, "Cramped living quarters and unexpected setbacks provoked the most even-tempered of household heads." And while racism and "oppression could bind a family tightly together," it could "also heighten tensions among people who had few outlets for their rage and frustration." Circumstances such as these, common across the nation, left young girls like Sarah at risk.

Whatever the nature of their home life, Sarah Breedlove did not stay with the Powells for very long. At the age of fourteen, Sarah married a man named Moses McWilliams and established a new household of her own. Even at the turn of the century, fourteen was young to get married. In the rural areas of the cotton belt, black men tended to marry at around age twenty-five while black women married at around age twenty. Still, while most Americans considered a fourteen-year-old to be young, few treated a fourteen-year-old like a child. Indeed, the age of consent was ten in much of the United States at this time. And perhaps Sarah found Moses McWilliams to be an especially attractive suitor. Whatever the case, sometime around 1881, Sarah Breedlove married and became Mrs. Sarah McWilliams. And Sarah McWilliams soon became a mother, giving birth to her daughter Lelia on June 6, 1885. Moses McWilliams disappears from the historical record shortly afterward, sometime around 1886 or 1887.

Despite the profound and transformative nature of these events, when looking back and describing this period of her life, Madam Walker would say simply that she was "widowed at twenty." But was she? As Hunter has shown, former slaves and members of freedom's first generation continued to make use of a range of marriage practices in the 1860s, 1870s, and 1880s, including "taking up" with each other in common-law unions that their community members recognized as perfectly legitimate. For those who had common-law marriages rather than marriages officially certified by the state, formal divorce was not necessary to dissolve the union. For a black woman who was no longer in such a domestic partnership and whose former partner had left the community, taking on the title of widow not only marked her change in status from a wife to a single head of household, it preserved her civil authority and ability to make contracts. It also preserved her respectability in the black community. Given this cultural context, it is certainly possible that Sarah and Moses McWilliams chose to separate and end their marriage and that Sarah chose to take on the title of widow.

But without evidence to the contrary, there is no reason not to take Madam Walker at her word. There were certainly many ways for a young black man to die in Mississippi in the 1880s. Perhaps he, like so many black Southerners, died of yellow fever or some other fatal disease. The Mississippi native Ida B. Wells, a contemporary who went on to participate in activist organizations alongside Madam Walker in the 1910s, lost both of her parents in the region's yellow fever epidemic of 1878.

Perhaps Moses McWilliams was killed by local white supremacists or official agents of the law. The decades between 1880 and World War I saw a marked increase in antiblack violence, with the extrajudicial execution, commonly known as lynching, of black men and women becoming a standard feature of Southern Jim Crow culture. Between 1880 and 1950, white Southerners lynched approximately five hundred people of African descent in the state of Mississippi. These gruesome, sometimes public, executions served as forms of terrorism against the black population. Given this climate, Moses McWilliams could certainly have fallen victim to antiblack violence.

Perhaps Moses McWilliams was arrested for some minor infraction and quickly tried, convicted, and sold as a forced laborer to a white plantation or mine owner without ever being given the opportunity to let his young wife and child know where he had gone. Perhaps, like so many black Southerners caught up in the South's emergent convict-lease system, he was worked to death and buried in an unmarked grave. Whatever the reason for his disappearance, be it death or departure, it is clear that by 1887, Sarah McWilliams, much like 20 to 25 percent of urban Southern black women between the years of 1880 and 1910, identified as a widow. Once again on her own, and now with a daughter to support, Sarah needed to assess her options.

With her brothers Alexander, Owen Jr., and James having already picked up stakes in Vicksburg and moved on to St. Louis, Missouri, it made sense for Sarah to join them and to begin to remake her life in a new city. So some-time in 1887 or 1888, Sarah made the journey to her new home.

As would be the case with most African American women who migrated out of the South, Sarah relied upon a phenomenon that historians have long called chain migration to keep their families intact. Just as immigrants from Europe did in the period, black Southerners moved to the same cities, neighborhoods, and buildings as their (usually male) relatives who had already established a foothold in the new city. This pattern persisted well into the twentieth century. Black women who left the South headed straight to their family and kin.

Sarah and her brothers were, once again, at the leading edge of a new phenomenon. Between the 1870s and 1910, roughly six thousand black Southerners moved to the cities outside the South every year. Like the Breedlove siblings, most began by exchanging their rural plantations for life in a nearby small town or city like Vicksburg. And like the Breedloves, many soon moved on to larger cities outside the South. In the 1910s, this trickle of black migrants suddenly became a flood, with hundreds of thousands of African Americans moving to the urban areas of the North and Midwest. Called the Great Migration, this demographic shift transformed the nation. But in the 1880s, Sarah and her brothers were simply the harbingers of the demographic revolution to come.

Black Southerners didn't just migrate *to* places. They also migrated *away* from places. And during the 1870s and '80s, many migrated to escape forms of antiblack violence. Vicksburg was one such city. Black Americans left Vicksburg at a significant rate in the decades after the Civil War. The city had been the site of the Vicksburg Massacre in December 1874, when white paramilitary groups murdered scores of African Americans in an effort to purge the last remaining black officeholders from their positions in municipal government. These White Liners, as they often called themselves, would police any behavior they deemed a threat to their white supremacy with vigilance and violence. For those black Southerners willing to take a gamble and migrate out of the South, leaving Vicksburg seemed like a reasonable risk to take.

St. Louis, meanwhile, appeared to be a reasonable place to go. Since the 1870s, St. Louis served as an important destination for migrants departing Vicksburg. In the years immediately following the end of Reconstruction, a charismatic man named Pap Singleton began exhorting followers from Louisiana and Mississippi to follow his lead to Kansas in search of land, opportunity, and freedom. Between 1879 and 1881, roughly twenty thousand rural black Southerners left their homes in the Deep South and headed for freedom in the "promised land" of Kansas. Known as Exodusters, these migrants gathered in villages across Louisiana, Mississippi, and other states, making their way to larger towns and cities like Vicksburg. From Vicksburg, these westward migrants took the ferry to St. Louis, the city billed as "the Gateway to the West." For these Exodusters, St. Louis signified the Red Sea, marking their passage out of bondage in the South to the promised land of freedom and landownership in the West. From St. Louis, the migrants continued on their way to Kansas, sometimes homesteading and creating all-black towns. Those migrants who couldn't afford passage all the way to Kansas found jobs in St. Louis, hoping to earn the money they needed to continue their journey to the West. Of these new arrivals, most ultimately ended up making St. Louis their new home.

Although Sarah and her siblings weren't part of the Exoduster movement of 1877, they did travel this well-worn migrants' path. Alexander Breedlove left Vicksburg for St. Louis in 1880. Owen and James made the journey soon after, arriving before the end of 1882. Although Owen later left St. Louis to head out west on his own, Alexander, James, and Solomon remained in the midwestern city. By 1883 the Breedlove brothers had established their own business as barbers. Thus, by the time twenty-year-old Sarah and baby Lelia arrived in St. Louis, the Breedlove siblings had put down roots in their St. Louis neighborhood. The siblings all lived within eight blocks of each other, near St. Paul African Methodist Episcopal Church.

For young women like Sarah, a bustling metropolis like St. Louis offered a wealth of opportunities and possibilities for a new life. While Vicksburg must have certainly seemed like an extraordinary change from the quiet, isolated, rural life of Delta, Louisiana, Vicksburg was a regional hub with a population that hovered around 12,000 year after year. St. Louis, however, was another matter altogether. At the time Sarah arrived in the city, St. Louis was a young metropolis of 450,000 residents and the fifth largest city in the nation (after New York, Chicago, Philadelphia, and Brooklyn). A city rife with a palpable sense of optimism for the new century, St. Louis exemplified all the possibilities, contradictions, and limitations of modern American life. A city in the midst of a noticeable transformation, St. Louis was expanding rapidly in terms of population and area. New neighborhoods and subdivisions sprung up outside the pre–Civil War city core, pushing the boundaries of the city westward. By the 1880s, homeowners, landlords, and municipal authorities embraced new technologies, installing electric lights inside buildings and replacing the old dim, flickering gas lamps that had once guarded city streets with new bright electric streetlamps. Public transportation—cable cars in the 1880s and electric trolleys in the 1890s—made it possible for the city's denizens to move from home to places of work and leisure with ease and speed. The decade also saw the emergence of the first early "skyscrapers." Multistory buildings of ten floors or more, skyscrapers ferried inhabitants from floor to floor via elevators powered by electricity. These new buildings popped up in the city's downtown district, cementing St. Louis's stature as a modern American city. By 1900, the city's population was 575,000, and it was the perfect site for the World's Fair of 1904.

Still, like other large northern and midwestern American cities in the period, St. Louis was a city of contrasts. This was especially the case for black residents of the city, who were increasingly confined to segregated neighborhoods with clear and firm racial boundaries. Like other black migrants to the city, Sarah McWilliams moved into the black working-class neighborhood downtown. And as she had done in Vicksburg, Sarah began working as a laundress. She was not alone in this enterprise. Indeed, more than half of the black women in St. Louis worked as washerwomen.

But like other black urban communities at the turn of the twentieth century, St. Louis also contained a diverse black population. Indeed, Sarah would have encountered the "old settlers" of St. Louis: African Americans who had been in the city for generations and felt themselves to be much more urbane, modern, and perhaps even more respectable than new arrivals like Sarah. These old settlers had spent decades creating institutions such as churches, mutual aid societies, and schools for their black community. They maintained a working relationship with a select group of white residents that dated back to the antebellum era. They also marshaled their resources to assist Exodusters and other migrants as they passed through or settled in the city in the 1870s. Given their big-city bona fides and, in some cases, free lineage, these old settlers sometimes took a critical stance toward migrants like the extended Breedlove family. The criticisms voiced by old settlers certainly reflected anxieties about their own status in a border state that was embracing emerging Jim Crow legislation and mandating separate educational facilities for black and white students. As the city's racial caste lines deepened, old settlers who once had boasted business and personal alliances with important white residents of the city found their social status declining precipitously. At the same time, however, segregated neighborhoods bound together all African Americans irrespective of education, income, or family background. And despite the fact that they may have sometimes looked down up on the accents, manners, dress, and comportment of their "country cousins," old settlers ultimately incorporated the Southern migrants into their growing black community. They also provided much needed services for new arrivals like Sarah McWilliams.

Like many black women migrants in the period, Sarah both benefitted from and contributed to the community-building and philanthropic work that black women routinely engaged in during the period. Upon her arrival in the city as a young widowed mother, she enmeshed herself in the institutions of St. Louis's black community, soon joining St. Paul AME Church. Founded in 1841, the church served as a central institution for black St. Louis. As a member of St. Paul's, Sarah also participated in the Mite Missionary Society, an organization that raised money for community members in need. Sarah also belonged to the Court of Calanthe, the women's auxiliary to the Knights of Pythias. Well on its way to becoming one of the largest black fraternal organizations in the period, the Knights and the Court of Calanthe served as a mutual aid society for their members and contributed to broader community initiatives.

Sarah also made use of the services black community organizations provided. The St. Louis Colored Orphans Home was one such institution. Founded in 1888 by an African American woman named Sarah Newton Cohron, the St. Louis Colored Orphans Home was one of many "old age homes" and orphanages that college-educated African American women established in black communities across the country at the turn of the nineteenth century. Established to ensure that the most vulnerable members of their communities were cared for, these institutions performed invaluable services in an era with few state-supported institutions for African Americans. In Sarah's case, the Colored Orphans Home provided the support she needed to establish a foothold for herself and her young daughter. She enrolled young Lelia as a "half orphan," a status that allowed her to leave Lelia in the care of the orphanage's matrons while she plied her trade as a laundress. The staff at the orphanage also helped Sarah enroll her daughter in their kindergarten as soon as Leila was ready to attend school. And in 1890, Leila graduated to first grade at Dessalines Elementary School, an institution closely linked to the Colored Orphans Home and named in honor of a leader of the Haitian Revolution.

As a migrant who relied on organizations such as these for help, Sarah may at times have felt a sense of distance between herself and the African American women who founded and staffed such institutions. She was, after all, a poor laundress and a migrant from the Deep South, while they were educated women in a position to dispense aid. At the same time, however, the black voluntary and community associations that Sarah engaged with—whether as a recipient of aid or as a member and fellow organizer—ultimately fostered a greater sense of community and connection between African Americans across class and generational lines. The very name Dessalines, for example, gives us a sense of the political consciousness of those who sustained St. Louis's black institutions. By choosing to name the school after the revolutionary Haitian leader Jean-Jacques Dessalines, the black residents of the city underscored the diasporic political consciousness and the communitarian political sensibility motivating black institution builders in the period.

These institutions sustained and gave a sense of purpose to countless African American women, and they remained important for Sarah as she weathered the loss of her brothers over the next decade. Alexander, the oldest Breedlove brother, died in 1893. James passed away in 1902. Owen, meanwhile, was now one thousand miles away. Sometime in the preceding years, Owen left St. Louis (and his wife, Samira) to carve out a new life for himself as a saloon owner and Republican Party booster in Albuquerque, New Mexico. Under these circumstances, a young single mother might find community associations essential for her personal well-being. For her part, Sarah McWilliams continued to maintain connections with black community institutions and organizations for the rest of her life.

Despite their omnipresent racism, cities like St. Louis also offered a wealth of opportunity for black self-fashioning and reinvention. In fact, these cities proved to be important sites of cultural ferment for African Americans. Segregated neighborhoods such as the ones the Breedloves called home housed black artists and entertainers, men and women who made these spaces incubators for the new, uniquely American expressive forms of the twentieth century: ragtime, jazz, and the dance crazes that accompanied them. St. Louis in particular was a wellspring of musical innovation. The neighborhoods of Mill Creek Valley and Chestnut Valley, where the remaining Breedloves moved in 1896, served as the home of jazz pioneer W. C. Handy, the composer of "St. Louis Blues."

For poor and working-class women like Sarah (who may sometimes have answered to the nickname "Sallie" in this period), urban leisure spaces offered a tremendous opportunity for self-fashioning. In less well-appointed jook joints, dives, saloons, and dance halls, laundresses and other domestic workers could drink, dance, and fraternize with friends after long backbreaking and demanding workweeks. Participating in black vernacular dances with names like "snake hips," "buzzard lope," the "slow drag," the "funky butt," and "ballin' the jack," men and women threw their arms around each other and pressed their bodies together, or scooted back and wiggled their hips suggestively according to the rules of the dance. Dressed in their most stylish outfits and free from the gaze of their white employers, young men and women could revel in the company of each other, appreciate their own beauty and bodily agency, and gain prestige in the eyes of their peers by demonstrating their skills on the dance floor. Accompanied by musicians playing the blues or ragtime, these young black men and women created the soundtrack of modern urban life and the expressive forms of modern American leisure culture.

Young Sarah McWilliams undoubtedly enjoyed the leisure culture of her new home. Indeed, she remained a fan of music throughout her life, making a point to champion black musicians years later at the height of her career as Madam C. J. Walker. Additionally, it may well have been in a space like this where Sarah met her new husband, a recent arrival to the city named John Davis, whom she married in a civil ceremony at St. Louis City Hall in 1894. The relationship lasted less than ten years. Although biographers have found no official divorce decree in the city records, John Davis appears to have moved out of the household and taken up with another woman by 1903. Affidavits filed when he swooped in to claim access to Madam Walker's estate after her death in 1919 described him as a violent, drunken, cheating husband.

Whether or not she found (or perhaps even lost) her husband at a music hall or a jook joint, Sarah McWilliams Davis certainly found that African American leisure spaces and community institutions served her well as she engaged in her own processes of self-fashioning. A major city like St. Louis offered young black migrant women from the country (who were part of a massive global movement of migration to urban areas) an extraordinary sense of autonomy and personal freedom. In fact, young, rural and working-class women from a range of racial and ethnic backgrounds seized upon these opportunities and began remaking themselves as modern American women. These self-fashioning efforts often felt extraordinarily empowering for this generation of new arrivals to the city. And they were especially pronounced for Sarah, a black working woman in her midthirties who was, by 1903, living on her own, attending night school, and spending time with a charming and ambitious new suitor named Charles J. Walker.

It was sometime during this period that Sarah met another young black woman who moved to St. Louis in search of opportunity. Like Sarah, Annie Turnbo Pope was a migrant woman. But unlike Sarah, Pope was not a domestic from the Deep South. Born in Metropolis, Illinois, on August 9, 1869, Annie Turnbo (who would later be known by the last name Malone, the surname she adopted in 1914 after her marriage to her second husband, Aaron Malone) was born to parents who had been free black northerners before the

Civil War. According to her official public account of her early life, Annie enjoyed styling hair as a young girl and used her knowledge of high school chemistry to invent a formula for hair cleansing and conditioning products. After successfully selling her preparations to friends, family, and neighbors in Lovejoy, Illinois, she moved to St. Louis in 1902. Known as Mrs. Annie Pope at the time, she began hiring black women as agents to go door-to-door and demonstrate the benefits of her "Wonderful Hair Grower." Mrs. Pope's Wonderful Hair Grower proved to be a hit—both with the women who purchased the product and received her scalp treatments and for the women who supplemented their family income by signing on to be one of Pope's agents and selling her products to their friends and neighbors. Sometime around 1903, Sarah became one of these women, receiving a treatment from Pope and subsequently joining her team of agents.

Sarah became a Pope agent at a particularly opportune time, for American women across the nation were beginning to rethink their relationship to beauty culture at the turn of the twentieth century. After 1890, new beauty ideals, first introduced by stage actresses like Sarah Bernhardt, who pioneered new ways of moving and posing, emerged to challenge older nineteenth-century American ideals about "natural" beauty. Mainstream advice writers increasingly emphasized the importance of using hair and makeup to enhance one's natural beauty. Meanwhile, by 1900, American magazine editors, department store owners, and advertisers targeted women as coveted consumers, steering them toward a paradise of products that promised to enhance every aspect of their lives.

African American women also bought into these emerging patterns of beauty and consumption, albeit on their own distinct terms. Elite and aspiring black women in particular often conceptualized beauty culture in political terms, claiming beauty culture not simply as individuals, as historian Noliwe Rooks points out, but also because of the prevailing belief that "how such women appear in public bears not just upon her, but upon her family, her friends, and indeed, the entire African American race." As the prominent black clubwoman Mary Church Terrell put it in "What the Colored Woman's League Will Do," published in the May–June 1893 issue of the black women's magazine *Ringwood's Journal*, "Every woman, no matter what her circumstances, owes it to herself, her family, and her friends to look as well as her means will permit." Elite and aspiring African American women often shared the idea that fashion could serve as a form of "armor that proved to the outside world (both African American and white) that the wearer, while an African American servant, was still a woman deserving of respect."

Working-class black women making a new home for themselves in cities like St. Louis may not have shared the exact same idea of how one should look her best. But new arrivals to urban areas (who were disproportionately poor and working-class) were often determined to leave behind their rural habits and adopt new fashions signifying their new urban status. For them, fashion may have served as a way to mark themselves as people who belonged in their new homes, these cities that appeared to offer a wealth of liberating possibilities.

In this new cultural climate, with modern beauty culture ascendant and new arrivals to the city seeking to throw off their country roots and style themselves as modern, twentieth-century urban women, Pope and her agents had a ready market. Here, they could tap into black women's community networks and associations as they went door-to-door, demonstrating, marketing, and selling hair-care products by and for black women. In this way, selling beauty culture as an agent for Mrs. Annie Pope offered black women a path toward a new type of freedom and liberation. Such possibilities must have felt especially exciting for women like Sarah. In addition to supplementing her income as a domestic worker, the job offered a set of financial opportunities outside the boundaries of white-controlled economic and social structures. The independence that came with the business of beauty culture, positioned as it was outside the purview of white men and women and black men, must also have felt both subversive and empowering. It also must have felt unequivocally modern.

Women like Mrs. Annie Turnbo Pope and Sarah McWilliams Davis may not have been homesteading on the great plains like the Exodusters who passed through the city of St. Louis years ago on their trek to Kansas. But they were pioneers nonetheless. And in 1904, both of these women stood on the precipice of remarkable personal transformations. Indeed, they would soon part ways and become lifelong business rivals. Beginning in 1906, Mrs. Annie Turnbo Pope officially registered her products under the trade name Poro and went on to expand her door-to-door business and grow her product line into a successful empire. Sarah McWilliams Davis, meanwhile, embarked on a parallel path beginning in 1905, heading out to Denver, Colorado, as an agent for Pope and beginning to fashion herself anew, this time into Madam C. J. Walker.

CHAPTER THREE

~

Madam Walker

In 1905, Sarah Breedlove McWilliams Davis left St. Louis, Missouri, and headed to Denver, Colorado. Her decision to relocate to the Mountain West was an unusual move for an African American woman at the turn of the twentieth century; the vast majority of black migrants from Louisiana and Mississippi chose to start their new lives in the towns and cities of the Upper South or the Midwest. But Sarah certainly wasn't the only black American in the period to make the trek westward. The West played a role in the black imagination just as it did in the white imagination at the turn of the twentieth century. And some black Americans saw the West as a region where they might find true freedom. Toward these ends, African Americans put down roots in the western territories and states for decades. A significant number of African Americans followed the overland trail to California during the Gold Rush era of the 1850s, many hoping to strike gold and make enough money to purchase the freedom of family members who remained enslaved. It was this ongoing quest for freedom that had inspired Pap Singleton's Exodusters to make the journey to Kansas in 1877. Black regiments of Union soldiers, often called Buffalo Soldiers, manned forts in Arizona and Colorado after the Civil War. And cities like Los Angeles and Denver contained a small but thriving black presence. As minorities in the Mountain and Far West at the turn of the twentieth century, African Americans existed in a frontier space where racial hierarchies from the southern and northeastern United States collided with racial hierarchies established under Spanish and subsequently Mexican rule before the territories became incorporated into the United

States. In these spaces, where legally mandated and casual forms of discrimination divided Anglo migrants from Chinese immigrants as well as Mexicans and Native Americans who had lived in the region for generations, men and women of African descent navigated inconsistent and ad hoc Jim Crow practices as they carved out livelihoods and communities for themselves.

Sarah's older brother Owen Breedlove epitomized these black pioneers. Although he moved along with his siblings as they migrated from Delta to Vicksburg to St. Louis, Owen broke away from his brothers and sisters and struck out for the Southwest in 1883. Ending his relationship with his wife, Samira (who remained with the rest of the Breedloves in St. Louis), Owen eventually settled in Albuquerque, New Mexico. There, he married a woman named Lucy Crockett, opened a saloon, and served as an active member of the Albuquerque Colored Republicans. Together, Owen and Lucy Breedlove would have four daughters—Anjetta, Thirsapen, Mattie, and Gladis. The family remained together in New Mexico until sometime around 1901, when Owen, having either moved on again or died, left his wife and daughters on their own. That year, the western Breedlove women relocated to Denver, Colorado, a city of more than 140,000 at the base of the Rocky Mountains. In 1905, Sarah decided to join them.

As she had done in the past, Sarah, now almost thirty-eight years old, moved in with family members, boarding with her sister-in-law and nieces until she found her footing in her new city. She soon found work as a cook in a boarding house, making about thirty dollars a month in wages. She joined the local AME church and began making lasting connections with members of Denver's small but vibrant black community of approximately 4,000.

Unlike her moves to Vicksburg and St. Louis, however, Sarah did not have to rely solely on the income she earned as a domestic. This time around she supplemented the low pay she received as a cook with money she earned providing hair-care services and selling Mrs. Annie Pope's Wonderful Hair Grower. She also pooled her earnings with those of her new partner in life, Charles Joseph Walker. A newspaperman who, like Sarah, had quite a bit of entrepreneurial spirit, Charles embraced the emerging leisure and consumption patterns of the young twentieth century, capitalizing on them whenever possible. Soon after his arrival in Denver in late summer 1905, Charles opened the Industrial Real Estate Loan and Rental Company with his partner B. W. Fields and began promoting raffles and popularity contests (one of many such proto-beauty contests sweeping the nation at the start of the twentieth century) and large-scale excursion parties for the city's black community. Sarah and Charles stood before a minister in a friend's parlor and married in January 1906. And within the year, Sarah began an unprecedented personal transformation.

Sarah would spend the next five years in motion, traveling around the country and relocating from Denver to Pittsburgh to Indianapolis. It was during this five-year period that she became an entrepreneur, first establishing herself as a beauty culturist with her own product line and beauty shop, and subsequently a businesswoman with a growing list of agents and her own manufacturing company. This rapid rise from domestic worker to industrialist took place in tandem with a carefully calculated personal transformation, for it was during this same period that Sarah Breedlove McWilliams Davis Walker remade herself into a new woman known as Madam C. J. Walker. This process involved far more than a change of name and some entrepreneurial spirit. It required a deliberate and multifaceted process of self-fashioning and attention to what twenty-first-century American marketers might call "branding." As she crafted her professional persona, Madam Walker also articulated a new narrative about the place of beauty culture in African American women's lives. By engaging in these two processes simultaneously—personal self-fashioning while reframing the cultural politics surrounding black women's beauty culture—Madam Walker created a new identity for herself and a unique brand for her company. Indeed, within less than a decade, the name Madam C. J. Walker, her life story, and her eponymous products would all be synonymous and interchangeable in the minds of black Americans. This popular version of Madam C. J. Walker resonated with a growing number of black women consumers eager to participate in modern beauty culture.

When she married Charles Walker in January 1906, Sarah was still an agent selling the product line of Mrs. Annie Pope. But within six months, Sarah severed her connection with Pope and became an independent beauty culturist. It is difficult to determine how she came to make this change in her life. Like other beauty culturists who built business empires in the period—Elizabeth Arden, for example—Sarah buried the details of her life experiences, personal relationships, and family history under layers of official company biographies and promotional materials. But we can assume that several circumstances may have influenced her decision to strike out on her own. Perhaps, as some scholars have suggested, her new husband, Charles (a man who appears to have been brimming with ideas for business schemes at this point in his life), encouraged her to make this move. Perhaps the suggestion came from a client or one of the other black women in her social circle. Perhaps, as biographer A'Lelia Bundles has suggested, the soon-to-be-famous pharmacist Edmund L. Scholtz (who may have resided at the same board-inghouse where Sarah was employed as a cook) analyzed the hair products Sarah planned to sell, presenting her with the list of ingredients so that she might order and prepare the products herself rather than selling Pope's line. Perhaps it simply became clear to Sarah that a western city like Denver, with its smaller percentage of black residents and paucity of black beauty cultur-ists, would be an excellent location for an enterprising woman to build up her own sizeable independent client base. Whatever the case, a thousand miles from St. Louis and far from Pope's oversight, Sarah now clearly felt free enough to do as she saw fit.

She appears to have made this leap during the first half of 1906. First, she created a new professional persona. Sarah initially advertised her services in Colorado's black newspaper, the *Statesman*, under the name Sarah Mc-Williams. But sometime around March 1906, she began placing ads in the *Statesman* under the name Madam C. J. Walker. Taking on the honorific Madam or Madame was a shrewd move for a woman in her line of work. The name Madam sounded European and conjured up a world of elegance as well as female authority and gravitas. The term signified her maturity and mar-ried status, which conferred respectability on both her person and her work. And, perhaps most importantly, Madam or Madame (both of which were used to refer to her in the period) was also the title of choice for women in the burgeoning beauty industry. According to historian Kathy Peiss, "White beauty culturists often shed their names, hometowns and social backgrounds to create personae as beauty experts. In a business dedicated to illusion and transformation, they were self-made. Madame Yale was, in fact, Maude May-berg," and "Ida Lee Secrest . . . [became] Madame Edith Velaro." In keeping with this tradition, Sarah Walker now stepped out into the world as Madam C. J. Walker.

By that time, Madam Walker also mixed and packaged her own product. In an era when black male scientists like George Washington Carver and Ernest Everett Just were making important strides in in the laboratories of the academy, black women like Mrs. Annie Pope and Madam C. J. Walker were making their own scientific discoveries in the kitchen. In doing so, Madam Walker likely built on and refined the formula used by Pope and the other product creators of the period. Both Pope and Madam Walker used ingredients like coconut oil and sulfur in their products; Madam Walker now added capsicum and other stimulants to the mix, giving her products a tingling sensation on the scalp.

That summer Madam Walker began pushing her rebranding effort even further. In July she placed a new advertisement reflecting her changed status in the *Statesman*, advertising her skills as a beauty culturist and advertising her own preparations. Choosing the name "Madam Walker's Wonderful Hair Grower" for her product, she then traveled to the nearby towns of Pueblo, Colorado Springs, and Trinidad to sell her wares and corner the state's market on black women's hair products. By August, Madam Walker had returned to Denver to open a salon for in-house treatments. Meanwhile, her daughter Lelia arrived in Denver to help with the fledgling business. Lelia, now a young woman at twenty years of age and a graduate of a St. Louis "hair growing" course, as these hair-care lessons were known at the time, prepared to help her mother expand the new family business enterprise.

Unsurprisingly, Mrs. Annie Pope found this entire turn of affairs to be less than ideal. After word of Madam Walker's new business venture made its way back to St. Louis, Pope responded by writing a public letter denouncing Madam Walker. Printed in the *Statesman*, the letter sought to reestablish Pope's place as the preeminent "hair grower" in Colorado's black community. To reclaim her territory, she soon dispatched a new agent to the area. Later in 1906, Pope chose a new name for her system of products, trademarking them under the name Poro. From her home in St. Louis, Pope (who would be known as Mrs. Annie Malone after her second marriage in 1914) went on to build Poro into a remarkable business empire. She and Madam Walker remained competitors and rivals.

But by the late summer of 1906, Madam Walker had already decided to move on. It had been just one year since her arrival in Denver, and in that time, she had accomplished a great deal. She established herself as a successful beauty culturist, with a product of her very own and a community of women who appreciated the way that she ministered to their needs. Perhaps she decided to cede some of this territory to her old mentor. Perhaps, feeling confident that she had a superior product, she felt ready to try to claim for herself a larger share of the market. The vast majority of people of African descent in the United States—roughly 90 percent—remained in the South at the start of the twentieth century. A clear-eyed entrepreneur, Madam Walker saw this as fertile territory filled with a new generation of young women consumers ready and willing to try a new beauty regimen at the start of a new century. So, in September 1906, the still-newlywed Walkers left Lelia in charge of their Denver salon and headed off for a promotional tour of the Southeast. During this period, the woman once known as Sarah Breedlove further refined her professional identity as Madam C. J. Walker.

During their seven-state tour across the South, the Walkers settled into a set of practices that Madam C. J. Walker would continue to follow in her many subsequent tours of the country. They located an African American hotel or family that took in boarders and they reached out to black church and community leaders. Madam Walker then offered a group demonstration of her hair-care process to local women. Available accounts suggest that Madam Walker's multistep process remained similar to Pope's emergent Poro hair care system. Both of these beauty entrepreneurs pioneered the concept of the beauty system; rather than peddling a single all-in-one product, Pope and Madam Walker sold several products and explained how to apply them in a step-by-step process to achieve a finished look. First, Madam Walker demonstrated how to properly massage the scalp and cleanse and treat the hair. She finished the process by using a light dressing oil and either curling the hair with strips of cloth or combing the hair with a steel comb that had been heated on a stove. After giving her demonstrations and collecting orders for her products, Madam Walker sent the orders back to Lelia in Denver for fulfillment. Lelia, in turn, mixed the ingredients, packaged the products, and mailed them to the customers.

To sell her Wonderful Hair Grower, Madam Walker had to market more than just her products. She also had to promote herself. In addition to demonstrating the steps in her hair-care system, Madam Walker had to explain who she was and how she came to do this work. To do this, she crafted a narrative about her entrance into beauty culture. Although the details of Madam Walker's early years as a hair culturist were surely more complicated than she preferred to share with the public, we can use her official origin story to gain insight into the larger cultural significance of her work. In later years, when describing how she came to be a beauty culturist, Madam Walker simply stated that her business began with divine inspiration: After years of toil as a laundress and domestic worker, her own hair began to thin and fall out, that "a big black man" or "African" appeared to her in a dream with a list of ingredients that she quickly ordered, and that her new preparations not only prevented further damage, but also caused her own hair to flourish. (Madam Walker's official history, company promotional materials, and newspaper profiles do not mention her work as a Poro agent for Mrs. Annie Pope.) It is a compelling tale, one that we can imagine her relating to rapt audiences of black women across the nation.

Let us leave aside her dream for the moment (we will return to this later). If we take Madam Walker at her word, it is certainly possible that her own hair loss might have inspired her to experiment with various ingredients and create her own hair-care formulas while she lived in Denver. Poor and working-class black women had few options for hair-care products in the late nineteenth century, often using harsh products like lye soap that could wreak havoc on fragile tresses. Indeed, Pope claimed that when they first met each other in St. Louis, Madam Walker initially suffered from severe hair loss that Pope's treatments ultimately cured. The stress of her daily life may also have taken its toll. Twenty-first-century psychologists have noted that stress can contribute to hair thinning and breakage. Given the turn-of-the-century context in which Madam Walker and black women like her lived, we can surmise that the backbreaking labor required of domestic servants as well as the stress of daily racism and other personal challenges might certainly lead to hair loss. Moreover, Madam Walker easily might have experienced a new bout of hair loss and breakage after her move to Denver. Breakage can often be a challenge for extremely coily hair even under the best of environmental circumstances. With its mile-high altitude and notoriously dry mountain air, Denver lacks the humidity that fragile, curly, and coily strands of hair often require to retain moisture, elasticity, and strength. Given these circumstances, the sudden transition from humid St. Louis to Denver may well have been a shock to Madam Walker's own hair, a stressful environmental change that Pope's Poro system may not have been able to address. Whatever the case, by 1906, Madam Walker believed she had created a superior product, one that she could sell on her own terms. And her ability to embody her tale of a woman who had cured herself of a common ailment surely resonated with the women she encountered as she traveled throughout the South.

In addition to embodying her own cure, Madam Walker also tapped into the cultural practices she learned during her first four decades as a child of the Mississippi Delta, a domestic worker, and a migrant. First, just as black women's hair care had been for generations, Madam Walker's demonstrations often became communal social events, taking place in domestic or semidomestic spaces such as kitchens or backyards. The women in attendance not only watched and listened to Madam Walker's tutorial but also responded to her and interacted with each other. Like the meetings of the church auxiliaries to which black women often belonged, these gatherings drew upon and strengthened bonds between women.

Possibly the best description of these events comes from Mamie Garvin Fields, who supplemented her income as a teacher with work as a Poro agent. Since both the Poro and Walker methods used similar techniques, Fields's description is worth quoting at length. Mamie Garvin Fields and her good friend Mamie Rodolph both learned the Poro method from a church friend (who, in turn, had learned the system from the wife of a local pastor). First, they experimented on each other's hair:

> We tried out the Sayman soap mixture, the sage rinses, the egg rinses, the pressing oil, the hair-growing pomade, and the special finger movements to make thin hair grow. They worked, too. One of the rinses was supposed to make dull hair "brilliant." So I told my sister Ruth, who had dull brown hair, and when we put on the sage rinse with egg yoke—oh, goodness! It did the trick.

After practicing long enough feel confident in their abilities, they sought out customers: "We took a long streetcar ride that ended up at Mt. Pleasant Street, where there was a big neighborhood of black people. With our two-burner oil stove and our hot combs, we got off the car and went to the first house: our turn to lecture now. So we explained how the system would improve the hair, and how we wanted to come up there on certain days to take care of the ladies' hair." She continued, "When we worked on the first ladies, the neighbors came to watch, so we worked out of doors the first time, under a tree. Very shortly we had that whole neighborhood, and then we had the next one. We got so many customers until we had to build something to hold them. Finally, Mamie and I set up chairs in our own home and let the people come to us."

These moments where one could relax with friends and take pleasure in one's own body and physical beauty facilitated individual and collective black well-being at the turn of the twentieth century. These communal events also had their roots in cultural practices of self-care developed over centuries of enslavement. Contending daily with a system that encouraged whites, both rich and poor alike, to assert some manner of authority over all aspects of black life, these affairs, along with dances, church services, and other celebrations, served as moments where black Americans repudiated the nation's racial caste system by claiming their bodies for themselves. To put it another way, it was in spaces such as these that African Americans relaxed in a world of their own making, one free from the white gaze and untrammeled by the racial caste system that shaped their workaday lives. Here in these spaces, black women created empowering rituals that took joy in their own beauty rather than privileging the standards of others.

As a hair culturist with a curative system, Madam Walker also took on a role akin to a healer. She consistently described herself as a hair "grower," telling anyone who asked that "I grow hair." This too placed her in a longer tradition of black women's cultural practices. For centuries, enslaved black healers, root doctors, and conjure women served an essential function in the South, caring for a variety of illnesses and ministering to the members of their communities. By framing her services as a form of bodily care, Madam Walker placed herself in this healing tradition, an appealing move that surely resonated with those women who left community healers behind as they moved from rural areas to larger towns and cities both within and outside the South. The services Madam Walker and other black hair culturists provided, then, can be understood as a new phase in a longer tradition of black women's healing practices. Indeed, Madam Walker's impulse to attribute her formula to the divine intervention of a "big black man" or "African" who appeared to her in a dream strengthened this connection to a centuries-old culture of healing rituals. More than an attempt to claim an authentic connection with the African continent, this portion of her dream must also be understood as a link to ancestral cultural practices and conjurers who helped men and women of African descent navigate the Americas. This aspect of her story further enhanced her authority with clients, agents, and prospective customers, allowing them to entrust her with the care of their bodies.

Madam Walker's system served as an especially appealing form of care for women who labored under difficult circumstances and whose bodies bore the scars of their years of toil. Twenty-first-century scientists have described the effects of trauma, systemic racism, and daily discrimination on the body. We should consider the possibility that these women, just a generation removed from slavery, living in a violent Jim Crow nation, and often migrants to a new region employed in backbreaking and low-paid domestic labor, might also have carried the scars—both psychological and physiological—of these experiences. If we keep in mind this context, we must also consider that time with a hair culturist like Madam Walker, often in the company of friends and neighbors, might feel physically and emotionally restorative. As someone who had spent forty years laboring under the same difficult conditions, suffered from similar illnesses, *and* developed a cure, Madam Walker ministered to these women simultaneously as an expert and a sister. This certainly enhanced her appeal as a beauty culturist.

Madam Walker's framing of her hair-care practices appears to have been well received by the women she encountered, for her travels through the South proved to be quite successful. By the end of the 1906, Madam C. J. Walker, a woman who had been earning less than $400 a year just two years earlier, had earned more than $1,000 in annual income. Her income continued to grow at a rapid pace as she and Charles sought a new place to settle. By the end of 1907, Madam Walker's business boasted $3,652 in sales receipts. Around the same time, the Walkers decided to move to the Pittsburgh.

When the Walkers arrived in the winter of 1908, Pittsburgh was an established industrial city. Home to the steel mills of Andrew Carnegie, Pittsburgh factory workers manufactured more than half of the steel produced in the United States every year. The city also contained glass mills and factories that built electric machinery, such as the parts produced in the Westinghouse factory. Pittsburgh was a thriving city of immigrants, one where recent arrivals from Eastern Europe and Russia worked twelve-hour shifts on the factory floor overseen by the children and grandchildren of immigrants from Ireland and Germany. The black population, meanwhile, began to tick upward, with African American arrivals from Virginia, Kentucky, and other Southern states now joining the population of old settlers whose parents and grandparents resided in the city as free blacks before the Civil War.

Once again, Madam Walker, now accompanied by her husband Charles, found herself part of a wave of black migrants. Between 1900 and 1910, the black population of Pittsburgh increased by 23 percent—from just under 18,000 black residents to just over 24,000 black residents—as African Americans continued to migrate in search of jobs and opportunity for a better life. This stream of African American migrants joined the tidal wave of European immigrants; Pittsburgh's total population grew from 321,000 to 534,000 in that same decade. Given the massive scale of European immigration, the black percentage of Pittsburgh actually declined in the first decade of the twentieth century—from 5.3 percent to 4.8 percent of the total population. Still the very presence of black Southern migrants touched off a sense of panic among the white workers of the city, who barred black laborers from joining their unions. European immigrants and their children, ever concerned about their own tenuous connection to whiteness, resented their proximity to black Southerners who, like European immigrants, relocated to Pittsburgh in search of a better life. In these years, Pittsburgh's once slightly permeable color line grew firm, continuing to harden in the coming decades.

Still, for Madam C. J. Walker, Pittsburgh seemed like an excellent location to grow her business. Located in western Pennsylvania, Pittsburgh served as a vital transportation hub, allowing easy access to all parts of the country. The city appeared to have few black hair culturists, so Madam Walker needn't wrangle for clients or compete against well-known competitors. And the city did have a well-established black middle-class with its concomitant clubs and associations. In other words, much as St. Louis had been two decades earlier, Pittsburgh looked very much like a place for Madam Walker to fashion herself into who she sought to become. So early in 1908, the Walkers moved into a home on Wylie Avenue in the black neighborhood of town. Soon afterward, Madam Walker opened shop at 139

South Highland Avenue in the fashionable East End, home to other elite and aspiring middle-class African Americans. Lelia soon joined them. The family opened a salon and continued to grow the mail-order business, which, by 1909, which earned Madam Walker nearly $9,000.

By 1910, however, the Walkers decided to move on again, choosing Indianapolis as their new home and the headquarters for the business. A city of 233,000 with a black population of just over 20,000 at the start of the decade, Indianapolis, Indiana, seemed like a fine city for Madam Walker to put down roots, produce her goods, and continue to expand her mail-order business. A midwestern railway hub that claimed "the Railroad City" as its nickname, Indianapolis served as a gateway to the South, the Midwest, and the Northeast, making it an attractive choice for a manufacturer who hoped to distribute products nationwide. The city also contained a growing number of black institutions, including the Afro-American Realty Company of Indiana and the American Home Buying Company, as well as two black-owned newspapers, the *Indianapolis Freeman* and the *Indianapolis Recorder*. Confident in her prospects and secure in her decision to build her business in Indianapolis, Madam Walker purchased a large twelve-room house at 640 North West Street in July 1910 for $10,000. Behind her new home, she would soon begin building her factory.

That year, she brought in more than $10,000 in income. With her mail-order business flourishing, Madam Walker began the process of building a state-of-the-art factory to produce her line of products. By late 1911, she claimed to have more than 950 agents selling her products across the country. Madam Walker was, by any measure, an extraordinarily successful entrepreneur. Her business was now a national enterprise, reaching across the United States.

Still, if she were to continue to expand her enterprise, Madam Walker now needed to establish a national reputation. With so few role models to guide her, Madam Walker had to draw from several streams as she forged the persona required to correspond with her successful brand and growing business. To help with this endeavor, Madam Walker embarked on an intensive advertising campaign. She used this campaign to market her products and to further acquaint the public with her brand and her persona, an identity commensurate with her expanding business enterprise.

Madam Walker developed an advertising campaign, in part, to overcome long-standing anxieties about the morality of beauty culture. For much of the nineteenth century, male African American leaders warned their listeners about the dangers of all aspects of beauty culture. In this sense, they echoed the edicts of the nation's white moralists, who worried about "confidence men" and "painted ladies" during the Victorian era. Early nineteenth-century American advice literature urged women to remain chaste and pure, linking these ideals with emerging middle-class ideals of women's natural beauty. In this context, artifice, in any form, was considered to be an indication of a woman's immorality and lack of respectability. These pronouncements found less currency with young American women, who, for the most part, embraced the rise of commercial beauty culture at the end of the nineteenth century. But despite this national paradigm shift in American consumer culture, many black American moralists and reformers continued to issue warnings about the dangers of beauty culture well into the twentieth century.

African American ministers and reformers considered cosmetics to be especially problematic, for the stigma of the "painted lady" held its own set of racial connotations. European and white Americans had long characterized women of African descent as sexually promiscuous, criminal, amoral women or, in the antebellum South, as deceitful jezebels who led supposedly virtuous white Southern men down the path to promiscuity. These characterizations shored up proslavery ideology before the Civil War, and now served as arguments for Jim Crow laws and its accompanying extrajudicial violence against African Americans. One of the more famous examples of these discourses in action occurred in 1895, when James Jacks penned a letter denouncing the antilynching activism of Ida. B. Wells. In her role as the editor of a black Memphis newspaper called *Free Speech*, Wells wrote an editorial condemning the lynching of her close family friend Thomas Moss, a man the white citizens of Memphis murdered, Wells explained, because they resented his prosperous grocery business and his competition with white grocers. Jacks attempted to discredit Wells, and, by extension, any effort to critique whites who lynched black Americans, by characterizing Wells as an immoral woman. As a woman of African descent, Jacks argued, Wells was inherently vicious and hypersexual, the antithesis of an ideal white woman. She was, in short, like any black woman, a person to be dismissed and ignored. Jacks's letter reverberated beyond Wells; elite and aspiring black women responded by organizing a nationwide club movement that unified under the auspices of the National Association of Colored Women (NACW) in 1896. But negative perceptions of black women's sexuality remained widespread. Given this context, however, cosmetics remained a charged issue for black ministers and reformers, who worried that black women's use of such products reinforced negative white perceptions about black woman's vanity and sexual availability.

Moreover, some black reformers also insisted that black women's hair-care practices caused as much concern as the use of cosmetics. As they saw it, some hairstyles required artifice—exactly what black women should avoid. Although there appears to be no consensus on what precise practices to denounce, black reformers characterized an astonishing array of black women's hair-care practices as just as dangerous, degraded, and immoral as paint and rouge. Most importantly, they argued, black women should steer clear of any rituals that might be perceived as efforts to straighten their hair in imitation of whites. At the 1904 NACW meeting in St. Louis, Alabama delegate Cornelia Bowen took a stand against the traditional practice of hair wrapping. Calling the practice "foolish," she proclaimed that "God saw fit to make it kinky" and urged black women to abandon this centuries-old beauty ritual. Bowen ultimately turned her anti–hair wrapping stance into a crusade, organizing "Anti-Hair-Wrapping Clubs," at her Mt. Megis School.

While Bowen—who, judging by photos from the period, was a light-complexioned woman with long, slightly wavy hair and likely was able to achieve the popular hairstyles of the day without stretching or pressing her hair—clearly misinterpreted the purpose of hair wrapping as well as the deep African roots of the practice, she was on to something. As a clubwoman who, like other black reformers of the era, remained committed to changing white perceptions of black culture, Bowen must have been acutely aware of the frequency with which white Americans ridiculed black women's appearance and aesthetic rituals. The popular visual culture of the period—print advertisements and illustrations, political cartoons, and commercial packaging—consistently rendered women of African descent as the very antithesis of the white ideal of beauty in every conceivable way. In the soap and detergent advertisements of the period, marketers appealed to white consumers by linking blackness with dirt and filth, implying that after use of the advertised product, even deviant blackness would be replaced with an idealized form of whiteness. Meanwhile, advertisements for beauty products manufactured by white-owned companies denigrated the physical features most commonly associated with African heritage. A product called "A Wonderful Face Bleach and Hair Straightener" promised to "turn the skin of a black or brown person four or five shades lighter, and a mulatto person perfectly white." The hair straightener in the box "is enough to make anyone's hair grow long and straight." The "before" and "after" drawings included in the advertisement illustrated the remarkable transformation promised by the product. Advertisements such as these defined white beauty ideals in direct opposition to black women. They consistently cast black women as undesirable, imperfect, and incapable of achieving beauty.

Additionally, a range of consumer products relied on images of servile blacks, tapping into a growing national nostalgia for slavery and the antebellum era. In the decades after the Civil War, as white Northerners and Southerners embraced popular literature and cultural events that promoted reconciliation between the regions, they also embraced the notion that ideal black Americans belonged in the rural South and exhibited docile, subservient behavior in keeping with the mythological representations of the Old South promoted by members of the Daughters of the Confederacy or in the fiction of Thomas Nelson Page or Joel Chandler Harris, or on the stage in the minstrel show or the popular "Tom Shows" of the era. In this formulation, African Americans remained preternaturally pastoral, rural, comic folk, at their best—picturesque even—when hard at work in the fields or serving the needs of whites. Indeed, whites regularly celebrated the "Old Time Negro" as superior to his descendants born after the war. By the 1880s, white Americans waxed especially nostalgic for the Mammy, invariably an older enslaved domestic caretaker who would have been incomplete without her iconic headwrap or scarf. Although enslaved women certainly labored as domestics within plantation households, white Americans celebrated a being more likely to exist in fiction than fact. As they saw it, the Mammy loved her subordinate position in white households. Consequently, she confirmed for them the genteel beauty of the Old South and the benign nature of its peculiar institution. This comforting message of white supremacy wrapped in a hazy layer of nostalgia proved remarkably popular with white Americans both North and South. Consequently, it appeared in a range of popular productions in the period, ultimately becoming ubiquitous across the American cultural landscape.

By the 1890s, this mythology received a heightened importance facilitated, in large part, by the expansion of advertising and consumer culture. In product after product, images of African Americans styled to resemble slaves serving masters adorned a range of advertisements and consumer goods—from shoe polish to thread to soaps and cleaning supplies to pancake mix. Products contained either grotesque caricatures of African Americans born on the minstrel stage in the 1850s or romanticized images of enslaved African Americans cheerfully catering to their owners' needs in the pre–Civil War South. These advertisements, which showed African Americans serving a leisured class of white Americans, harkened back to what whites remembered fondly as the "good old days" before emancipation, soothed white anxieties about a growing number of black migrants to the North and West, and tapped into the white consumer's desire for upward mobility. At every turn, the visual culture of the urban landscape insistently framed black

Americans as premodern, rural, and unfit for modern life and the full privileges of citizenship.

For black women, this imagery coalesced around one article of clothing: the headwrap. Whether on the stage, on the screen, or in print, the article of clothing used by white writers, actors, and artists to stigmatize black women as other, inferior, and unfree was the (invariably red) bandana or headwrap used to tie up black women's hair. In other words, in the hands of those creating mass American popular culture, an article of clothing that had, for generations, been essential to black women's communal hair-care practices and expressions of individual style became fodder for white amusement. Paired with text employing deliberate grammatical errors, malapropisms, and misspellings whites used to approximate "authentic" black speech, representations of black women in headwraps came to signify black women's bodily "difference" from white women and their close proximity to slavery. In this configuration, black women who happily cooked, cleaned, nursed, and otherwise cared for white families—and, moreover, had no desire for freedom of their own—offered a comforting image of the appropriate subservient role for black people in the United States. The image of Aunt Jemima with her iconic red headscarf—the figure that, by 1910, was synonymous with pancake mix—and the Mammy ideal upon which she was based became one of the most significant advertising images of the era.

Moreover, it was not just the bandana, but black women's hair itself that marked not simply difference, but deviance and inferiority. Popular minstrel tunes from the period, for example, regularly ridiculed the physical appearance of people of African descent. One such tune, "When They Straighten All the Colored People's Hair" critiqued black Americans' economic and political aspirations by lampooning African features. The lyrics of this jaunty little tune by Gussie L. Davis, published in New York in the 1890s, are worth quoting at length.

> Oh, you jolly little nigger,
> You make a funny figure,
> For your wool kinks up just like the letter "O,"
> And you seem to be so happy,
> Although your head is nappy,
> But, then never mind, 'twill not always be so;
> They have got a new invention, and they say it's their intention,
> To experiment on darkies ev'rywhere,
> Oh, your face it may be dark, but you'll be happy as a lark,
> When they straighten all the colored people's hair.
> Now the white folks keep a laughin',

And at you they keep a chaffin',
And the Irish call you "nigger" so you say,
But you has one consolation,
'Long as you has education,
You're as good as white trash any time a day;
Let me tell you how it happen' Cain and Abel got a scrappin',
And a curse was put on Cain and all his race,
Then his hair began to kink, right away, just only think,
Then they stamped old Africa upon his face.
Don't you darkies get excited,
Ev'ry wrong will soon be righted,
When you git up in de middle of the air,
Then you'll raise a big sensation,
Just like any other nation,
And the wind will blow the kinks out of your hair;
There must be some transformation,
Fare there's any emigration,
And the coon's commence to climb the golden stair.
Oh, you'll be a happy jap,
When your wings begin to flap,
When they straighten all the colored people's hair.
Refrain
When they straighten all the colored people's hair,
When they straighten all the colored people's hair;
Your nose, it may be flat, but you needn't care for that,
When they straighten all the colored people's hair.

As these lyrics suggest, American popular culture ridiculed blackness in multiple ways. In addition to the casual use of racial epithets, the song relied upon a representation of black hair as a distinguishing feature, one that underscored the difference and deviance of black bodies. This inferiority, in the logic of the song, was mandated by divine authority and thus could never be overcome. Furthermore, the song's underlying premise assumes that people of African descent wanted nothing more in life than to look, well, white. The song links hair straightening with black efforts to gain education and to advance in American society, making all such efforts seem ridiculous and doomed to fail.

For those black reformers who remained deeply concerned about the politics of the white gaze, black women's beauty efforts had the potential to give ammunition to those whites who viewed black Americans in this way and continued to ridicule African Americans at every turn. Given this context, changing one's curl pattern—no matter how mildly or temporarily—appeared to confirm all of the most insulting antiblack stereotypes of the era. Thus, by the start of the twentieth-century, African American women found the hair-styling practices of their enslaved grandmothers *and* the newly popular methods of hair-care promoted by women like Madam C. J. Walker initially denounced from a variety of quarters.

Over the next decade, Madam Walker deftly recast these dynamics in her public demonstrations. In her origin story, she made it clear that it was neither her African heritage nor a deficiency in natural beauty that caused her hair loss, but rather the hours she put in each week laboring as a washerwoman. Moreover, this same heritage ultimately saved her, for it was an African who came to her in a dream, giving her the recipe for her formula. Furthermore, Madam Walker's decision to frame her role as that of a healer rather than as one who sought to use artifice to change black women's appearance undercut these concerns for her customers.

Madam Walker's advertisements also stood in stark contrast to the period's prevailing antiblack imagery. Unlike the advertisements pushed by white-owned beauty companies that treated blackness like a disease to be cured, Madam Walker promised a version of black beauty bound up with race pride rather than aspirational whiteness. On February 12, 1910, Madam Walker first announced her arrival in the *Indianapolis Recorder*, proclaiming, "Mme C. J. Walker, of Pittsburg, Pa., THE NOTED HAIR CULTURIST is in this city at the residence of Dr. J. H. Ward" where "she will demonstrate the art of growing hair." Using the three-frame before-and-after photographs she would use in many of her advertisements over the next decade, Madam Walker tied black beauty to race pride, saying, "Every woman of pride should see her during her stay in this city." She then followed with a letter from ministers and prominent women and men representing the black communities of Pittsburgh, New York, and St. Louis, all attesting to Madam Walker's honesty, respectability, and skill as a hair culturist. The letter and the appeal to "every woman of pride" moved Madam Walker's products out of the realms of artifice and vanity onto what African Americans of the era understood to be political terrain. And she continued to seek the "patronage of every woman of pride who is in need of her services" in the coming years.

Madam Walker also linked her products with discourses of Christianity. An early 1910 advertisement included an eight-point section called "The Reason Why" where Madam Walker also noted that her products were effective because the recipe came to her "as an inspiration from God—through a dream." She would later turn the advertisement into a pamphlet to distribute to potential customers and supporters.

At the same time, however, Madam Walker also tapped into the modern language used by women reformers in the period, characterizing her work in the progressive discourse of health and modernity. In doing so, Madam Walker claimed new ground for her system of hair care. Madam Walker positioned her system—neither an effort to emulate the physical characteristics of white women nor an old-fashioned practice harkening back to the pre-emancipation days—as one that was modern, efficient, and healthful. She did this by tapping into the progressive politics espoused by black clubwomen of the day and characterizing her products as something that would help one successfully engage in the politics of respectability and enter male or white spaces as ideal representatives of their communities. Madam Walker also reflected the zeitgeist by acknowledging the concerns of the progressive women of the day who considered themselves to be "New Women." Finally, her advertisements emphasized hygiene and cleanliness instead of white beauty ideals. By embracing modern sensibilities while simultaneously nodding to black folk culture, Madam Walker created a bridge from a rural black past to a soon-to-be urban present for a new generation of black women consumers.

Finally, by naming her products after herself, Madam Walker claimed her authority to heal, packaging her knowledge for black women to purchase and use for themselves. To put it another way, when acquiring or enhancing their appearance with Madam Walker's eponymous products, black women also bought into Madam C. J. Walker's brand, personal narrative, values, and version of care. Madam Walker further strengthened this association by putting her own image on the packaging. In doing so, Madam Walker deepened the connection between her name, her story, her image, and her products. She also challenged prevailing representations of black women in Western consumer culture: Hers was not a picture of black servility; rather, Madam Walker represented brown-skinned natural beauty, health, independence, and well-being.

Over the next decade, Madam C. J. Walker continued to build upon this foundation. Armed with a new product, a new identity, and a modern advertising campaign, she now intensified her efforts to expand her business and promote her brand. From her new home in Indianapolis, Madam Walker went on to fashion herself into a businesswoman of extraordinary note, a manufacturer with a national reputation for her wealth and commitment to philanthropy. To do so, she turned to the most important network of African American women in the period—the National Association of Colored Women—and set out to gain the support of the gatekeepers, the tastemakers, and the most prominent men and women of the race.

~

CHAPTER FOUR

Businesswoman

Madam C. J. Walker arrived in Indianapolis in 1910 with a popular line of products and a growing base of customers. Now a reputable beauty culturist with a thriving mail-order business and a growing roster of agents, Madam Walker and her husband Charles settled in to their new Indianapolis neighborhood, purchasing and renovating a building at 640 North West Street. With construction completed by the summer of 1910, Madam Walker prepared to entertain guests in her "excellently appointed" home and hire workers for the neighboring factory. Sometimes called a "laboratory," in keeping with her desire to make a modern, healthful, scientifically sound product available to the public, Madam Walker's factory soon contained workers mixing and preparing Madam C. J. Walker's Wonderful Hair Grower. By 1911, Madam Walker employed more than thirty people on-site. She also hired two talented young black attorneys—Freeman Briley Ransom and Robert Lee Brockenburr, alumni of Columbia and Howard universities, respectively—to manage her business and legal affairs. With her business still less than a decade old, she had already become a force to be reckoned with.

On September 19, 1911, Madam Walker filed incorporation papers in the name of the Madame C. J. Walker Manufacturing Company of Indiana, worth $10,000 in capital stock and divided into one thousand $10 shares. Madam Walker, Charles, and Lelia comprised the entire board of directors, keeping the profits in the family. Lelia, having recently married and quickly separated from her first husband, John Robinson, soon left the Pittsburgh salon and joined her mother in Indianapolis. In an effort to drum up additional interest in the Walker system of products, Charles spent much of his time on sales trips through the South. Madam Walker, meanwhile, remained the undisputed head of the organization, overseeing all aspects of the enterprise.

Madam Walker's decision to make the Madame C. J. Walker Manufacturing Company a corporation was an extraordinary step on personal, professional, and political levels. That she chose to put her full name on the venture underscores her boldness and self-confidence as an entrepreneur. On a political level, the move to incorporate her business gave Madam Walker the kind of legal standing that African Americans—whether as individuals or as a group—rarely obtained in the United States. With incorporation, Madam Walker ensured that the rights of her company remained fully protected under the law. On a professional level, the move marked Walker's entrance into a rarefied circle, a small group of highly successful American women entrepreneurs.

These included a small number of black women who, like Madam Walker, embraced the name "businesswoman." For example, Madam Walker's primary rival Mrs. Annie Turnbo Pope Malone continued to expand her Poro company. Over the next few decades, Malone prospered in black St. Louis, where she built a beauty college and factory. Malone also supported a plethora of African American institutions and philanthropic causes during Poro's heyday in the 1910s and '20s. Her civic engagement made her a pillar of African American communities. In another line of work, Maggie Lena Walker turned an African American mutual aid society—the Independent Order of St. Luke—into a successful insurance company and bank for black Southerners. In 1903, Maggie Lena Walker chartered the St. Luke Penny Savings Bank, stepping into the role of bank president. In the coming decades, Maggie Lena Walker's bank acquired and merged with all of the other black-owned banks in the city of Richmond, Virginia.

Black women even sought to put their entrepreneurial spirit to work in the entertainment industry. Frustrated by the racist treatment and inequitable pay scale they encountered as performers on the vaudeville circuit, Emma and Mabel Griffin founded a theatrical agency for black performers in 1913 and quickly began leasing theaters for black vaudeville troupes who performed before black audiences. On April 4, 1913, the Indianapolis Freeman covered their act and entrepreneurial activities, calling them "ladies who did 'business' with a capital B." By 1914 and 1915, the Griffin Sisters reportedly earned roughly $200,000 annually (in early twenty-first-century values) between their business investments and their own performances.

Although the Griffin Sisters, Maggie Lena Walker, and Mrs. Annie Malone established very different businesses, each of them ultimately exhibited a hallmark of early twentieth-century African American entrepreneurship: a dedication to what was then often referred to as "racial uplift." Black Americans across the nation relied upon African American institutions and networks to help inspire and sustain each other in the midst of their political, economic, and social oppression in the United States. In addition to the churches, schools, and mutual aid societies that proliferated in the decades after emancipation, African Americans added a host of new newspapers, clubs, and professional associations at the local, state, and national levels. Even as de jure (required by legal statute) and de facto (customary) forms of Jim Crow segregation and discrimination expanded across the United States, black entrepreneurs worked with other members of their communities to expand and support this array of institutions and organizations. Whether they built their businesses in concert with members of a local mutual aid society, relied on preexisting women's networks, or created a new professional network of their own, black women entrepreneurs like Maggie Lena Walker, Mrs. Annie Malone, and the Griffin Sisters relied upon African American networks and community associations. They insisted that their business enterprises serve the needs of other African Americans. And they contributed to the expansion and growth of institutions in African American communities. For these businesswoman, entrepreneurship and uplift remained intertwined.

Like her contemporaries, Madam Walker embraced the prevailing uplift ethos. Indeed, much of her success in this period can be traced not just to her tenacity and skill in marketing and selling her product, but also to her ability to tap into the networks and traditions that sustained turn-of-the-twentieth-century African American communities. Madam Walker's efforts to engage these networks certainly facilitated the expansion of her business and the solidification of her brand. But her personal investment in black associational life also served as a means to express and enact her vision of uplift entrepreneurship. Between her arrival in Indianapolis in 1910 and the end of 1912, Madam Walker leaned into these networks. In the process she simultaneously embodied, challenged, and ultimately redefined the self-help and racial uplift strategies championed by the most powerful black American of the era, Booker T. Washington. She would end 1912 with the support of the most prominent leaders of these institutions as well as a new moniker: Madam C. J. Walker would claim the title "the foremost colored businesswoman in the world."

Even before she became a hair culturist, Madam C. J. Walker surely encountered the ideological perspective fostered in nineteenth- and early twentieth-century black community institutions and associations. Often referred to as the "politics of respectability," "racial uplift," or "black formalism" by scholars, this sensibility bound black Americans of varied regional and class backgrounds together through a shared set of beliefs and political goals that they reinforced for each other through the formal rites and cultural rituals regularly practiced in black schools, churches, clubs, and community associations. Closely intertwined with the Protestant work ethic, respect for education, and conservative sexual mores, this uplift agenda emphasized the creation of institutions, the inculcation of the skills and personal habits commensurate with upward mobility, and a commitment to the advancement of the collective status of black Americans in the United States and abroad. This ethos permeated black institutions during the late nineteenth and early twentieth centuries, shaping the worldview and identities of a range of black Americans irrespective of their educational background. Despite her lack of a formal education, for example, Madam Walker participated in the rituals of black formalism every time she raised her voice to join others in singing "Lift Every Voice and Sing" or supported an event sponsored by the churches she attended in Vicksburg, St. Louis, Denver, Pittsburgh, and now Indianapolis.

For the African Americans who embraced these ideals, the personal and the political remained inextricably intertwined. Moreover, most black Americans understood the values and day-to-day forms of behavior associated with "racial uplift" primarily in intra-racial terms: Education was valuable for its own sake and for training up the next generation, church served as a place for fellowship with one's neighbors and one's God, and black institutions sustained the health of black communities. At the same time, however, a number of African American elites and community leaders imbued these activities and mores with an additional ideological or political purpose: Representations of respectable behavior, they argued, should be disseminated widely and used to convince white Americans of black America's worthiness for the full privileges of citizenship. Viewing uplift strategies as a strategic response to the racism of the early twentieth century, elite and prominent black Americans from a range of political perspectives agreed on the central tenet of racial uplift ideology: Every black American—no matter their occupation or station in life—had the responsibility to fashion themselves into their ideal selves. Although this belief system would always be at odds with the forms of working-class black vernacular expressive culture that one might enjoy while dancing the "snake hips" at a jook joint on a Saturday night, this cluster of values defined black institutional and associational culture in the late nineteenth and early twentieth century.

As a child of freedom's first generation, Madam Walker grew up in the midst of this rapidly expanding black cultural ethos. Not surprisingly, she acted in accordance with this constellation of values as she expanded her business enterprise. Unlike some black elites, however, who obsessed about the white gaze, Madam Walker's primary interest in who viewed her as "respectable" remained an intra-racial rather than interracial concern. Rather than worrying about what white observers might perceive her, Madam Walker made certain that those African Americans around her—specifically black women and local black community leaders—considered her to be a respectable woman. During her time in Pittsburgh, for example, Madam Walker sought and received the endorsement of African American religious and secular community leaders, who signed a letter stating, "We, the undersigned, highly recommend Mme. C. J. Walker's work and worth." In addition to noting that "as a hair grower she has no equal," they further described her as a "strictly honest, thorough-going business woman." Madam Walker continued to seek this type of endorsement and cultivate this image throughout her entire career.

In addition to assiduously attending to her reputation, Madam Walker made it a point to focus on her own education and intellectual improvement. This effort became easier after she hired a woman named Alice Kelly to take the position of forelady at the Indianapolis factory. Madam Walker met with Kelly during a January 1910 trip to Louisville, Kentucky, and found her to have the skills necessary for the management of day-to-day operations at the factory. A recipient of a classical liberal arts education and proficient in Greek and Latin, Kelly taught at the Eckstein-Norton Institute in Kentucky. In addition to filling the essential supervisory role in the factory, Kelly served as Madam Walker's traveling companion and private tutor, helping Madam Walker to fill in the gaps in her education, improve her grammar and refine her penmanship, and in the process, prepare Madam Walker to navigate the most prestigious black networks and social circles. These types of self-improvement efforts had long been cultivated by elite and aspiring African Americans who saw education and other personal self-improvement efforts as part of a larger collective struggle for freedom in all its fullness. Like other elite and aspiring black Americans, Madam Walker embraced her education wholeheartedly, putting energy into this self-improvement endeavor even as she continued to expand and promote her business.

In addition to attending to her own education and seeking out the endorsements of respectable local black leaders, Madam Walker tapped into key African American networks. She began doing so by connecting with the leadership of the National Association of Colored Women. Founded in 1896, the NACW served as an umbrella organization for secular black women's clubs and facilitated black women's efforts to craft an independent agenda that reflected their unique needs and responsibilities as educated black women. As nineteenth-century American women who invested in some of the period's gender-specific notions of morality and domesticity, NACW members felt that they could help their people by "raising to the highest plane home, moral and civil life." As black women who, because of their race, their common heritage as descendants of slaves, and the persistent and pernicious racism they all faced, felt unified with people of African descent irrespective of class or region, NACW members insisted on staying in "close touch with the masses of [black] women" and planned to "inaugurate the reforms" that might help the poorest among them. In keeping with the uplift ideology that these women would ultimately be instrumental in refining, they chose "Lifting as We Climb" as their organization's motto.

Through their local clubs and state federations, the women of the NACW engaged in community-building work without the oversight of male ministers from African American churches or the white women who controlled national temperance, suffrage, and social welfare organizations. From its earliest days as an organization, the NACW focused on a range of topics members felt called to combat as African American women. Members raised funds to build and support orphanages, kindergartens, and old age homes in black communities. They also promoted education for young black women, fought against segregated transportation, denounced the rapidly spreading convict lease system, and campaigned against forms of antiblack violence such as lynching. As NACW president Mary Church Terrell put it, "We are daughters, sisters, mothers, and wives. We must care for ourselves and rear our families, like all women. But we have more to do than other women. Those of us fortunate enough to have education must share it with the less fortunate of our race. We must go into our communities and improve them; we must go out into the nation and change it. Above all, we must organize ourselves as Negro women and work together."

By 1901, the NACW had increased to more than seven times its original membership, claiming approximately three hundred clubs representing thirty states. By 1910, the organization had expanded exponentially, with state federations as well as local clubs. White women delegates from other national women's organizations, including the Young Women's Christian Association and the National American Woman Suffrage Association began lobbying the NACW, hoping to gain the organization's support for their programs.

The interracial leadership of the National Association for the Advancement of Colored People (NAACP), founded in 1909, also shared leadership positions with leaders of the NACW and utilized the NACW's community network to expand its own organization. Consequently, by the second decade of the twentieth century, the NACW was an essential African American institution and the premier organization for African American women.

Madam C. J. Walker certainly understood the political and cultural importance of the NACW long before her arrival in Indianapolis in 1910. In 1904, while she was working as a laundress in St. Louis, the NACW held its fourth biennial convention at Madam Walker's own St. Paul AME Church in St. Louis. Although there is no way to know if Madam Walker actually attended any of the open sessions or had the opportunity to hear any of the organization's leaders give a public address, her position as a member of the St. Paul women's auxiliary ensured that Madam Walker shared the responsibility for welcoming and hosting the two hundred NACW delegates from around the country. Moreover, the St. Louis delegation actually included two members of St. Paul: Lavinia Carter, a board member of the St. Louis Colored Orphans Home where Madam Walker boarded Lelia when they first arrived in the city, served as a delegate to the convention. Meanwhile, Maria Harrison, president of the Colored Orphans Home, attended in her capacity as president of the St. Louis Federation of Colored Women's Clubs.

As the premier organization for African American women, the NACW counted amongst its membership a number of prominent African American women. Its leadership and most notable clubs remained associated with the elite and middle-class women of black communities, women like past president Mary Church Terrell (the wife of a judge and the daughter of one of the first black millionaires in the United States) and Margaret Murray Washington (wife of Tuskegee Institute president Booker T. Washington). While most local NACW-affiliated clubs relied on more accessible indicators of respectable status—neatness of dress, high moral standards, and commitment to the health and well-being of their people—the leadership of the national body remained, at least at the turn of the twentieth century, more exclusive. These women were tastemakers and style influencers on a national level. Some of the organization's more famous figures achieved something akin to celebrity status within the organization. The early twentieth-century teacher and beauty culturist Mamie Garvin Fields later described to her granddaughter what it was like to listen to members of the NACW leadership. A member of the Charleston, South Carolina State Federation of Colored Women's Clubs, Fields recalled a time when Mary Church Terrell visited Charleston's Mt. Zion AME Church. As the first president of the NACW, Terrell was a famous clubwoman; she drew a crowd that "packed into the pews so tight until you had to put even the smallest purse on the floor, between your toes." Fields recalled that "all of Charleston was waiting to hear what Mrs. Terrell would say about the role of the Modern Woman. Oh, my, when I saw her walk onto that podium in her pink evening dress and long white gloves, with her beautifully done hair, she was that Modern Woman. And when her voice went out over that huge crowd . . . no one wanted to miss a word."

Madam Walker had not enjoyed the same educational opportunities that most leaders of the NACW received in their youth, but by 1910 she was a prominent black woman in her own right. Now, as an indisputably successful and respectable businesswoman, Madam Walker found herself well positioned not simply to participate in local NACW affiliated clubs, but to become part of the ranks of the organization's national leadership. And in the late summer of 1910, Madam Walker joined the delegation representing the Indiana State Federation and traveled to the NACW's biennial convention in Louisville, Kentucky. By linking up with this influential black women's network, Madam Walker expanded prevailing notions of who an elite black woman could be and what a laundress could become.

As an official state delegate to the NACW convention, Madam Walker had the opportunity to network with some of the most respected, politically engaged, stylish, and prominent black women in the nation. As she strategized and socialized with other NACW members, she increased her number of contacts, shared her story, and marketed her products. Some of the Indiana delegates, such as Mrs. Ora Day, already counted themselves among Madam Walker's list of clients, women whose healthy, resplendent heads of hair could serve as a testament to Madam C. J. Walker's expertise as a beauty culturist and an effective advertisement for her Wonderful Hair Grower. These women helped Madam Walker publicize her products and enabled her to secure her national reputation as a respectable beauty culturist. They also presented local networks for Madam Walker to tap into as she traveled across the country. Indeed, immediately after the convention, Madam Walker traveled eastward from Indianapolis to New York, stopping at women's secular and religious clubs to tell her life story and market her products. She would continue to collaborate with local, state, and national NACW figures as she established herself as a philanthropist and institution builder in her own right.

Madam C. J. Walker's transformation from beauty culturist to businesswoman took place during the golden age of black business enterprise and associational life. During this period, black institution builders viewed entrepreneurship as an individual endeavor with collective racial significance. Black entrepreneurs like Madam Walker understood that their success invariably required them to connect with and support the networks and institutions that knit together black communities across the United States. In keeping with this tradition, Madam Walker took steps to demonstrate her willingness to place her monetary success in the service of her people. Madam Walker's growing bank account and good standing among her peers made her uniquely well positioned to become a major contributor to black institutions and philanthropic efforts after her return to Indianapolis.

Although it is tempting to define philanthropy according to the example set by a few turn-of-the-century wealthy white male industrialists such as Andrew Carnegie and John D. Rockefeller, black Americans—both free and enslaved—had their own tradition of what we might consider philanthropy dating back to the early nineteenth century. In the years after emancipation, as freedmen and women began building churches and educational institutions across the nation, they often relied upon the members of their own communities to donate land and raise funds. Even in cases where wealthy white benefactors like Julius Rosenwald pledged substantial funds, local black community members still pooled their resources, raised money, donated materials, and contributed time and labor to build schools for their children in rural areas across the South. Additionally, elite and aspiring African Americans felt keenly the responsibility that came with their personal resources. As they saw it, they had a duty to do whatever they could to improve the collective status of people of African descent. Because the black philanthropic tradition was a community-wide phenomenon, rather than a simple top-down phenomenon that some might call "noblesse oblige," poor and working-class black women became well practiced in the art of mobilizing neighbors and raising funds to build the institutions that supported and sustained their communities across the nation. Thus, Madam Walker's relationship with philanthropy must be considered more than a simple desire to "give back," or an attempt to mimic the behavior of industrialists like Carnegie. Rather, Madam Walker's commitment to philanthropy grew out of a long tradition of African American community-building efforts.

Like most poor and working-class black Americans at the turn of the twentieth century, Madam Walker connected with black philanthropy through much of her adult life, receiving aid and contributing to philanthropic causes long before she became a beauty culturist. During her years as a young migrant and single mother, she and Lelia relied upon institutions created by the black women of St. Louis. As an active member of her AME church in St. Louis, Madam Walker undoubtedly participated in this burgeoning culture of black philanthropy and community engagement. Indeed, later in her life Madam Walker would look back on her years in St. Louis and say that it was there in her church where she spearheaded her first fundraising campaign, raising money to help a blind and impoverished member of their community as well as others in need. As a popular hair culturist and member of the AME church in Denver, Madam Walker also surely remained cognizant of local community efforts. And when NACW president Margaret Murray Washington visited the city and gave a series of lectures to the small black community by the Rocky Mountains, Madam Walker may well have connected their local efforts with the larger national NACW agenda. In other words, the culture of giving and sense of collective responsibility nurtured during the heyday of black associational activity was as much a part of Madam Walker's sense of self as her entrepreneurial spirit and hard-nosed business sense. This cultural perspective shaped her attitude toward philanthropic giving throughout her career as a businesswoman.

Madam Walker's opportunity to demonstrate her commitment to black institution building arrived in 1911, as philanthropists in Indianapolis embarked on a campaign to build a new Young Men's Christian Association (YMCA) building for the city's black community. The branch of the YMCA set aside for the city's African Americans could no longer accommodate the number of young men and boys who attended the various educational and religious programs of instruction or took part in the basketball games and other forms of physical fitness activities. So in October 1911, wealthy white philanthropists kicked off a fundraising drive to build a new "colored branch" of the YMCA in Indianapolis. They chose October 20 as the date for the official start of the fundraising campaign.

Two days before the formal campaign began, Madam Walker publicly pledged to donate $1,000 to the building fund. Madam Walker's biographer A'Lelia Bundles writes that the "symbolism of her gift challenged all conventional wisdom about black women and wealth in early-twentieth-century America." The sizable gift put Madam Walker in the ranks of the wealthy white male donors who organized the fundraising effort. The gift also showcased Madam Walker's keen marketing sensibilities, for she understood that such a large gift—given by a black businesswoman—would generate talk in many quarters, thus promoting interest in her system of products and increasing her name recognition in black households across the country. It truly was a staggering amount of money for her to pledge. And the move made Madam C. J. Walker a household name in Indianapolis.

Contributing such a large sum also helped Madam Walker further her campaign to market herself and push back against those ministers and reformers who not only remained deeply suspicious of the beauty industry but also viewed beauty culture and those who practiced its arts or peddled its products as charlatans who endangered the political prospects of the race. Madam Walker's donation to the YMCA—an organization committed to nurturing and protecting the morality of young men—underscored her claims to be an honorable woman engaged in a reputable line of work.

Still, it would be a mistake to interpret Madam Walker's donation as a purely mercenary act. According to the logic of the black philanthropic tradition, her monetary contribution served as a demonstration of how one might dedicate one's resources to the greater good of black people. By publicly contributing such a large sum, Madam Walker claimed her place as a leader in the black community and a living personification of the uplift ethos. It was a bold and audacious move, especially for a woman. In making the gift, Madam Walker shattered expectations for what black women could achieve in business. Soon after this, Madam Walker began describing herself in her promotional materials as the "Best Known Hair Culturist in America."

Now if only she could get Booker T. Washington to pay attention.

At the turn of the twentieth century, Booker T. Washington was, without question, the most powerful black man in the United States. Known as the "Wizard of Tuskegee," Washington founded and presided over Tuskegee Institute in Alabama. Washington championed business enterprise and manual training, and he promoted agricultural and industrial labor for African Americans wherever he went, characterizing the steady acquisition of wealth as the best chance for the black population to gain independence and flourish in the United States. Much like Madam C. J. Walker, Booker T. Washington had experienced a remarkable change in circumstances over the course of his life. Born a slave in Alabama in the 1850s, Washington had been part of that first generation of Southern African Americans to receive more than a rudimentary education during the years immediately after the Civil War. While attending Hampton Institute, Washington distinguished himself as a model student, one who completely inculcated and thoroughly embodied Hampton's gospel of manual education and bootstraps philosophy of self-help. After teaching for a few years, Washington went on to found Tuskegee Institute. In 1895, Washington received nationwide attention after giving an address at the International Cotton Exposition in Atlanta, Georgia. Now known as the Atlanta Compromise speech, Washington implored the Southern white audience to employ black Americans as laborers.

In exchange, he suggested, black Americans would eschew efforts to regain the political rights they had lost throughout the South. Together, Washington vowed, black and white Southerners would work together as one hand while remaining as separate as individual fingers. This speech catapulted Washington to fame; whites viewed him as the national leader of the African American population and extended to him access to wealthy whites and political figures. Although Washington quietly supported civil rights lawsuits, publicly he adhered to his primary message for black Americans: Black entrepreneurship would serve as the best antidote to the racist caste system that restricted and disenfranchised people of African descent in the United States. Consequently, he advocated industrial training and encouraged black Americans to focus on building businesses. In doing so, he hoped that the entire race would soon follow the path he had forged "up from slavery."

As the most famous and powerful black man in the United States, Washington controlled key black institutions and networks. In addition to running Tuskegee Institute, Washington also had his acolytes installed in leadership positions in black organizations around the country. He controlled a number of black-owned newspapers. Serving as the representative of the black population, Washington had ties to President Theodore Roosevelt's White House between 1901 and 1909. Bankrolled by wealthy white philanthropists and titans of industry, Washington held unparalleled power and influence in elite African American circles, shaping the content of African American newspapers and deciding exactly who was who in black America. For black Americans, Washington was the ultimate gatekeeper. To truly establish herself as a notable businesswoman, Madam C. J. Walker needed Washington's blessing as well as his support for her brand.

In many respects, this should have been relatively easy, for Madam Walker acted upon the self-help values espoused by Washington. In fact, these values guided Madam Walker as she forged her own career trajectory, influencing her decision to hire Alice Kelly as a personal tutor as well as her focus on building her own business. Madam Walker pointedly referenced these themes in her personal statements early in her career. Take, for example, Madam Walker's entry in the 1909 Pennsylvania Negro Business Directory. The full-page description with photograph described Madam Walker as "one of the most successful business women of the race in this community. Madam Walker has established a reputation for her hair grower and pressing oil that extends throughout the country. Having made the treatment of the scalp a thorough study, she has successfully established a lucrative business. She treats persons by mail or at her well equipped parlors, 2518 Wylie Ave., Pittsburgh, Pa." In just a few short sentences, the ad highlighted points where Madam Walker aligned with Washington: her well-equipped (in other words, respectable) parlors, her knowledge of hair care gained through "careful study" (in other words, education, self-help, and hard work), and the fact that she had "successfully established a lucrative business." Given the paucity of successful black businesswomen like herself, Madam Walker expected to find a natural ally and supporter in Washington.

Unfortunately for Madam C. J. Walker, Booker T. Washington was not a fan of black women's beauty culture. Although he had no problem with African American men who worked in the barbering trade or opened barbershops for white customers, Washington remained deeply opposed to African American women's beauty culture. In fact, he went so far as to exclude black women hairdressers from his 1907 book, *The Negro in Business*, and allowed only two African American women hairdressers, both of whom catered to a white female clientele, to speak at his National Negro Business League (NNBL) conventions in 1901 and 1905. Historians have speculated about what drove Washington's opposition to black women's beauty culture. Blain Roberts, for example, surmises that "as a former Hampton student under the influence of Mary Armstrong, Washington probably opposed all modern beauty aids on moral grounds." Scholars have also suggested that Washington may have felt especially challenged by beauty culturists like Madam Walker because of their poor and working-class backgrounds. Neither of these possible attitudes deterred Madam Walker, however. Convinced of the worthy and respectable nature of her business, Madam Walker set out to garner both the endorsement of Washington and the favor of the National Negro Business League.

Beginning as early as 1910, Madam Walker made several attempts to meet the Wizard of Tuskegee. She reached out to Washington on January 19, 1910, telling him, "I have a Remedy, that will grow any kind of hair. It has been tested and proven to be the only thing that does not record a failure white and black alike." Revealing that her goods were "the product of a dream," she explained that she hoped to "form a stock company at a capital of five thousand dollars then we could sell shares and make this one of the largest factories of its kind in the United States, and would give employment to many of our boys and girls. I know that I can not do any thing alone so I have decided to make an appeal to the leaders of the race." Washington promptly replied the following week, politely declining to support her endeavor and wishing her success.

Later in 1910, Madam Walker learned that Washington planned to travel to Indianapolis as the keynote speaker for the meeting of the Knights of Pythias and its female auxiliary, the Court of Calanthe. Madam Walker wrote to Tuskegee, inviting Washington to visit her home and inspect her factory. But Washington did not accept her invitation and instead left the city the day after his talk. Moreover, Washington's secretary, Emmett Scott, responded dismissively to Madam Walker's written request.

Tenacious as ever, Madam Walker continued to reach out to Washington the following year. On December 2, 1911, Madam Walker wrote to Washington to let him know that she hoped to attend the Farmers Convention hosted by Tuskegee Institute in January 1912. She sent Washington her advertising booklet along with a brief note. She wrote:

> My Dear Sir: I am desirous of attending the Farmers convention which will convene at your school Jan. 17th, 1912.
> I am writing to ask if you will allow me to introduce my work and give me the privilege of selling my goods on the grounds.
> Enclosed please find my booklet which will give you an idea of the business in which I am engaged.
> Thanking you in advance for an early reply, I am, Yours respectfully,

> Mme C. J. Walker

Washington's response was less than welcoming. Soon after, Madam Walker received a disappointing reply from the Wizard of Tuskegee. In a letter dated December 6, Washington wrote:

> My dear Mme Walker: I have your kind letter of some days ago.
> I fear you misunderstand the kind of meeting our Tuskegee Negro Conference will be. It is a meeting of poor farmers who come here for instruction and guidance, and who have very little or no money.
> I am well acquainted with the business in which you are engaged, but somehow I do not feel that a visit to our Conference would offer the opportunity which you seem to desire.
> With kind regards, I am, Yours very truly,

> Booker T. Washington

Likely annoyed by Washington's condescending reply to her query, Madam Walker wrote back again in mid-January. This time, she defended herself, her good name, and her dedication to the collective black freedom struggle:

> Mr. Washington: I am writing you this note to ask if you will be kind enough to introduce me to this Conference. I do not want to explain my work, but I do

want them to know that I am in the business world, not for myself alone, but to do all the good I can for the uplift of my race, which you well know by the great sacrifice I made in the interest of the Y.M.C.A. of Indianapolis. I believe that if others knew of my great struggle from the age of seven years without any parents to assist me up to six years ago, when I entered the business arena at that time and having succeeded in building it up to where my income is now more than $1,000 per month, it would be a great inspiration to them to do likewise.

Trusting you will not deny me this one opportunity, I am: Obediently yours,

(Mme) C. J. Walker

As this letter demonstrates, Madam Walker squarely positioned herself as one who placed her business enterprise within the larger framework of racial uplift. She reminded Washington of what he surely already knew—that she donated a significant sum of money to a major fundraising campaign. And she claimed her own personal bootstraps narrative.

Again, Washington declined.

Undeterred, Madam Walker and her husband went to Tuskegee anyway. And when Madam Walker pressed the issue in person, she gained permission to speak briefly at an evening chapel session (although not during the regular conference proceedings). In addition to her convention remarks, Madam Walker took the opportunity to give demonstrations and treatments to eighty-four customers during her time at Tuskegee. Among these, according to biographers, were members of Booker T. Washington's own family. Over the course of the event, Madam Walker secured so many new customers and contacts that she decided to open an agency near the campus. She left the agency under the direction of an agent named Dora Larrie, a beauty culturist Walker had met and personally trained in Indianapolis.

The Walkers then embarked on another marketing tour. This trip included a stop at the NACW's biennial convention. Held in July at Hampton Institute in Virginia, the convention brought together NACW members from across the country. During the proceedings Madam Walker publicly volunteered to lead a fundraising campaign for fellow NACW member Mary McLeod Bethune's Daytona Normal School. These and other efforts earned Madam Walker a formal resolution of sincere thanks from the NACW for her work "to improve the appearance of our women" and her efforts on behalf or "race progress." This was the best stamp of approval that Madam Walker could possibly receive. Not only were these the most influential women reformers of the race, they were also often married to some of the most prominent black men of the day. This made the objections of male leaders like Washington increasingly futile. In addition to failing to recognize the commercial beauty trends sweeping the nation, these men seemed to have very little understanding of the aesthetic preferences and grooming practices of the women in their own families.

Later that summer, Walker arrived at the NNBL convention in Chicago. Founded by Washington in 1900, the NNBL focused on promoting black entrepreneurship in the United States. Once again, Washington refused to allow Walker to address the assembly, even going so far as to overrule an Indiana delegate's request that Walker be allowed to say a few words. At this point, Madam Walker had had enough. She rose from her seat exclaiming to Washington, "Surely you are not going to shut the door in my face!" Madam Walker then gave an impromptu address to the delegates and spectators, outlining her life experiences, defending her occupation, and proclaiming her will to be "Best Known Hair Culturist in America." As she told her story, she put forward a narrative that would soon become legendary. "I am a woman that came from the cotton fields of the South; I was promoted from there to the washtub . . . then I was promoted to the cook kitchen," she explained. She then pivoted from the passive voice "I was promoted" to the active voice, asserting her own agency and declaring "from there I promoted myself into the business of manufacturing hair goods and preparations." She did her work, she said, not simply for herself, but rather for the larger good of the race. And unlike those who might try to obscure their humble origins, "I am not ashamed of where I come from." Those present responded to her words with resounding applause.

This was a watershed moment in the life story of Madam C. J. Walker; here she succinctly articulated the "from the washtub to the boardroom" narrative that she would share with countless audiences until her death. By framing her story in this way, Madam Walker tapped into a long tradition of African American entrepreneurship as racial uplift. In the coming years, Madam Walker would communicate this ethos at every public opportunity, placing this narrative at the center of her personal story, her political activism, and her marketing campaign for the Madam C. J. Walker Manufacturing Company. In doing so, she consistently linked the personal with the political for black consumers.

Moreover, this was the moment when Madam C. J. Walker finally gained Booker T. Washington's stamp of approval. Pushed, perhaps, by the enthusiastic response of those assembled, Washington had no choice but to respond favorably to Madam Walker's compelling life story and her demonstrated commitment to her people. Madam Walker was, after all, a living embodiment of his own oft trumpeted ideology of self-help. Besides, his own wife,

Margaret Murray Washington, incoming president of the National Association of Colored Women, reportedly used Madam Walker's product line. Perhaps Booker T. Washington saw an opportunity to cultivate a new donor. Whatever the case, Washington subsequently invited Madam Walker to speak at the next NNBL convention in 1913. He also agreed to be Walker's guest during his next visit to Indianapolis.

Getting the blessing of Booker T. Washington made Madam C. J. Walker a major player in the world of black business leaders. But her ability to gain Washington's official endorsement also meant that Madam Walker had redefined the conception of self-help and uplift as defined by Washington. As a businesswoman who was a hair culturist, Madam Walker had created a successful enterprise catering not to white Southerners but to the needs of other black women like herself across the country. While Washington tended to focus on local enterprises, Madam Walker thought nationally. And by centering women's work and women's health, Madam Walker merged the uplift ethos of the National Association of Colored Women with the business and self-help philosophy of Booker T. Washington. In the process, Madam Walker helped to redefine for black Americans like Washington the parameters of what a black woman could be and do and become.

In December 1912, months after her return to Indianapolis, the *Indianapolis Freeman* underscored Madam Walker's status as a notable black business leader. Crowning Madam C. J. Walker as "America's Foremost Colored Business Woman," the newspaper published a profile of Madam Walker and the Walker Manufacturing Company. The piece outlined the company's history, touted the factory, and celebrated the woman behind the business, tracing Madam Walker's swift rise from poverty and obscurity to fame and fortune. Most significantly, the article made it clear that black Americans did not interpret Madam Walker's ascension to the status of America's foremost colored businesswoman simply as a Horatio Alger tale of pluck and luck or view her success through the lens of heroic American individualism. Rather, African Americans reveled in Madam Walker's achievement because they claimed her story as a symbol of their own progress as a people.

In just two years Madam Walker had achieved yet another milestone. Ultimately, through her philanthropy, her approach to black uplift entrepreneurship, and her commitment to black women's networks, Madam Walker managed to redefine and expand the parameters of the turn-of-the-century racial uplift ethos. In the coming years, she would continue to link the personal with the political. But now she began taking on a new set of challenges, and in the process, crafted a new identity for herself. By 1912, Madam C. J. Walker was well on her way to becoming a modern race woman, one who moved beyond the racial uplift approaches of the previous generation and embraced the more radical, confrontational, and daring forms of political engagement that heralded the emergence of the radical black politics of the early twentieth century.

CHAPTER FIVE

~

Race Woman

The year 1912 had been an extraordinary one for Madam C. J. Walker. She received the endorsements of the National Association of Colored Women and Booker T. Washington's National Negro Business League. A major African American newspaper crowned her "America's Foremost Colored Business Woman." And the Madam C. J. Walker Manufacturing Company continued to expand its profits and its product line. By 1913 Madam Walker brought in $3,000 per month in income. The company now sold a range of products including Glossine, Vegetable Shampoo, Temple Salve, Tetter Salve, Wonderful Hair Grower, and a steel hot comb that straightened hair much like the twenty-first-century flatiron. Madam Walker's business was, in no uncertain terms, a success. With her eye toward the future, she made plans to build a beauty college and purchased property in New York City.

At the same time, Madam Walker experienced a number of changes in her personal life. In October 1912, Madam Walker divorced her husband Charles, severing all legal ties between them. Sometime in the preceding months, Charles became romantically involved with Dora Larrie, the Indianapolis agent Madam Walker hired to oversee the expansion of the business in Tuskegee, Alabama. Charles quickly took up with his new love interest, leaving Madam Walker to return to Indianapolis on her own and decide how to proceed. Years later Charles would write a letter apologizing profusely for his behavior, but in 1912, he was excited by the prospect of a new beginning with a new partner, and he and Larrie set off to start their own competing and short-lived hair product line in the South.

Madam Walker was now forty-five years old and well acquainted with love and loss. Barely out of girlhood when she lost her first husband in Vicksburg, Mississippi, she had also experienced a brief marriage with John Davis in St. Louis before she married Charles Walker in 1905. But Madam Walker's sense of self did not rise and fall on her marital status. And she now stood at the helm of a thriving business that, by all accounts, appeared to have tremendous opportunity for further expansion. She had "promoted herself," as she put it, "from the washtub to the boardroom." If Charles wanted to leave, then he could go. It was the dawn of 1913, a modern age. And Madam Walker was a modern woman with a vision. She had work to do. She would focus on enlarging her business empire.

Although Madam Walker bid farewell to her husband in this period, she also gained a granddaughter. In late October 1912, Lelia Walker Robinson adopted a young girl named Fairy Mae Bryant. (Fairy Mae would later legally change her name to Mae Walker Robinson.) The daughter of a local widow named Sarah Etta Hammond, Fairy Mae worked as a "young girl solicitor" for the Walker company, running errands and doing other light work. She also had a full head of long, dark hair, the kind of hair one would expect to find on the head of a descendant of the foremost hair culturist of the race. Hammond, like any mother, must have weighed heavily the proposition of giving her child up to another family. Still, Lelia Walker Robinson was the daughter of the woman who was known as "America's Foremost Colored Business Woman." In this context, giving up her daughter for adoption into the Walker family likely seemed like an extraordinary chance to change Fairy Mae's life and improve her prospects for the future.

As Madam Walker continued to grow her business, she began to actively integrate the political sensibilities of the day with her brand. This was a multipronged strategy that involved unifying and professionalizing her agents, further refining her marketing strategies, expanding her global outlook, and increasing her philanthropic activities. Each of these efforts went hand-in-hand with her own political sensibilities. Indeed, Madam Walker often found herself participating in activist campaigns alongside the most prominent African American activists in the era. And for the rest of the decade, Madam Walker embraced the growing range of African American political engagement, drawing upon a diasporic perspective, entertaining new forms of radicalism, and privileging the perspective of the working classes over those of the elite. For these reasons, Madam C. J. Walker would come to exemplify the modern race woman.

The term "race man" first appeared in the nineteenth century and became an increasingly important part of the black political lexicon as new forms of political engagement redefined black activism in the United States during the early decades of the twentieth century. Although the term "race woman" appeared with less frequency than "race man," Madam Walker clearly embodied the spirit of the term long before it came into daily use in African American communities. As a race woman, Madam Walker centered the perspective of working-class black women. She also supported increasingly direct forms of civil rights activism while at the same time remaining committed to black institution building. Finally, Madam Walker put forward a political project that was simultaneously aesthetic as well as political, and moreover, accessible to the many rather than the few.

Over the course of the decade, Madam Walker embraced the heightened spirit of activism sweeping African American communities. The 1910s saw a flurry of new forms of activism; more African American activists embraced a growing range of alternative ideological frameworks and created new organizations to fight for the rights of people of African descent. This process accelerated after Booker T. Washington's death in 1915. Meanwhile, white antipathy and violence toward African Americans continued to deepen in the early decades of the twentieth century, driving black Americans from the South and threatening them in the cities of the North and Midwest. Indeed, the era saw a marked increase of spectacles of antiblack violence across the nation. These circumstances underscored the need for a multifaceted program in pursuit of change. Madam Walker's relationship with activism exemplified these developments.

For example, despite her persistent pursuit of Booker T. Washington's favor, Walker also connected with Washington's biggest political rival, W.E.B. Du Bois. The first African American to receive a PhD from Harvard, Du Bois was a pioneering sociologist, historian, and civil rights activist. He had achieved fame with his 1903 essay "Of Mr. Booker T. Washington and Others," a piece that challenged Washington's Atlanta Compromise speech and put forward two key counterarguments: that black Americans should fight for their civil and political rights and that those who were best suited to do so should pursue an education in the liberal arts. A founder of the Niagara Movement, Du Bois formed an alliance with progressive whites and founded the National Association for the Advancement of Colored People in 1909. The NAACP remained dedicated to the fight for African American civil rights into the twenty-first century.

Madam C. J. Walker and W.E.B. Du Bois first began consistently moving in each other's orbits sometime around 1912. Madam Walker began advertising her company's products in the NAACP's magazine, the *Crisis*.

As editor of the *Crisis*, Du Bois surely maintained some familiarity with the young magazine's roster of advertisers. *The Crisis*, meanwhile, also covered Madam Walker's philanthropic endeavors, including her contributions to the YMCA and her plans to establish a school in South Africa.

Although Madam Walker never established an institution on the African continent, her public declarations of her intent to do so signal another aspect of her political perspective: her diasporic consciousness. In late 1913, Madam Walker left for a trip to the Caribbean and Central America. She spent two months in the region, traveling to Jamaica, Haiti, Costa Rica, Cuba, and the Panama Canal Zone. Madam Walker was accompanied by Anjetta Breedlove, her niece from Colorado, who had become something of a traveling companion for her. Madam Walker also traveled with the famous singer Madam Anita Patti Brown and her entourage of black musicians.

On what was simultaneously a business and a leisure trip, Madam Walker sought to explore the region for a number of reasons. As a businesswoman, Madam Walker surely hoped to cultivate new markets. At the same time, however, she felt compelled to assess what life was like for African-descended men and women in the Caribbean and Latin America. Clubwomen like Madam Walker often expressed concern for their Caribbean neighbors, especially in the wake of the American occupation of the nation of Haiti. As an active member of the NACW, Madam Walker would have been very interested in assessing life in Haiti and other Caribbean nations. The trip gave her an opportunity to engage directly with women of African descent outside the United States. As she did so, Madam Walker took the opportunity to begin building a roster of agents and a clientele in the Caribbean. This, in turn, had implications for how black women in the Americas understood each other. Historians have shown that consumer culture served to forge global connections between women of African descent in this period. By establishing some of these earliest connections, Madam Walker helped to facilitate the emergence of modern black women's internationalism.

Upon her return to the United States, Madam Walker took steps toward further cultivating black women consumers across the Americas. During her stay in New York City in June 1916, she wrote a long letter to her business manager and attorney, F. B. Ransom. In the midst of several clarifications about the status and destination for orders and requests for canceled checks and financial statements, she asked Ransom to "please send me some Spanish books. I have a Porto Rican [sic] here who is taking the trade. She is going back home to open a Parlor and would like to take some literature with her." By tapping into these diasporic markets, Madam Walker laid the groundwork for new cultural affinities between black women in the hemisphere.

In addition to demonstrating an interest in the prospects of people of African descent in Latin America and the Caribbean, Madam Walker also turned to the courts in an effort to defend her civil rights. In 1915, Madam Walker filed a lawsuit against the Central Amusement Company, the owner of Indianapolis's Isis Theater, requesting damages after an incident of blatant racial discrimination. The new theater had been open for barely one year and boasted seats for eight hundred patrons. As a "five and ten cents" establishment, the theater charged viewers five or ten cents for a ticket. On February 20, 1915, Madam Walker went to the Isis Theater to catch a "moving picture show." However, when she arrived and endeavored to "pay the usual, customary, and advertised price," the agent refused to sell her a ticket. Instead, he demanded "twenty five cents [sic]," saying "that was what colored people would have to pay to see the said show."

In seeking to charge Madam Walker more than twice as much for her ticket, the theater agent engaged in a fairly common American form of racial discrimination. On one hand, the agent could assume that when faced with such an exorbitant fee, most black Americans would be unable—or simply refuse—to pay such a price. In this way, he had the power to create and enforce the establishment's arbitrary color line. Alternately, whenever African Americans decided to cough up the price of the ticket, the corporation profited handsomely from it. This tried-and-true formula had long shaped real estate transactions in the North and the Midwest. Even in the decades before the Civil War, landlords in Northern cities charged black tenants more than their white counterparts. Famous photographer and reformer Jacob Riis remarked on this tendency in the late nineteenth century, noting that landlords in New York City found black tenants to be cleaner and more stable than "lower grades of foreign white people" yet charged them higher rents for the same accommodations. This pattern intensified as increasing numbers of African Americans relocated to Northern cities during the first decades of the twentieth century. Given this history and context, the Isis Theater seemed to be applying the racist economic logic of accommodations to public amusements.

As a black woman in the United States, Madam Walker certainly experienced racism before her negative encounter at the Isis Theater. She'd learned to negotiate it as a girl growing up in Louisiana and Mississippi. She'd watched antiblack officials roll back the post–Civil War political gains of the Reconstruction era and she'd grown into adulthood during the rise of the violent, regressive, racist oligarchy of the Jim Crow South. As an active member of black churches and community organizations, Walker had likely attended countless secular and religious meetings where those present hammered out a strategy for pushing back against Jim Crow while simultaneously taking collective steps to build up their community from within. These experiences sharpened Madam Walker's understanding of the workings of American racism. They also shaped her sense of justice. And as a race woman with the means to fight back, she intended to do so.

Madam Walker filed suit against the company that owned the theater, claiming that the corporation and its theater agents violated Indiana's civil rights laws. Her suit referenced Indiana state law noting that "all persons within the jurisdiction of the state of Indiana, shall be entitled to the full and equal enjoyments of the accommodations, advantages, facilitie [sic] privileges of inns, restaurants, eating-houses, barber shops, public conveyances on land and water, theaters, and all other places of public accommodations and amusements, subject only to the conditions and limitations established by law and applicable alike to all citizens of every race and color and regardless of color or race." Aware that the defendants were likely to invoke racist stereotypes about black women's lack of refinement and respectability in an effort to call her character into question, Walker stated that "when she applied for a ticket and admission to said show, she was clean, sober, neatly dressed, and orderly, that she was ready and willing at all times to comply with all lawful and reasonable rules and regulations of said defendant corporation." She asked for $100 in damages. How the case was resolved remains lost to the archive. We do know, however, that Madam Walker did go on to build her own theater, which was completed after her death.

Even if Madam Walker failed to win $100 in damages, her lawsuit had meaning. In filing suit against the Central Amusement Company, Madam Walker joined the ranks of other race women in the era. For decades, black women turned to the courts and sued when their rights to equal public accommodations were curtailed, whether by individuals or the state. Elizabeth Jennings successfully sued for being barred from a streetcar in New York City in 1854. In the 1860s, the entrepreneur Mary Ellen Pleasant filed two successful lawsuits after being denied access to San Francisco streetcars. Her case resulted in the desegregation of the city's streetcar system. Even when they were unsuccessful, lawsuits such as these were part of a collective history of African American activism in the nineteenth and twentieth centuries. While still a young teacher, Ida B. Wells sued after being violently ejected from the ladies car—or first-class car—of a railroad, despite having purchased a first-class ticket, in 1883. Although she initially won damages, the Tennessee Supreme Court overturned the verdict in 1885. Like Homer Plessy, whose ill-fated antidiscrimination lawsuit ultimately reached the Supreme Court in the form of *Plessy v. Ferguson* in 1896, black women turned to the courts in an attempt to beat back the rising tide of racism. By standing up to racism and filing her own lawsuit, Madam C. J. Walker embodied the modern race woman. She also nurtured this spirit in her agents.

Throughout her career, Madam C. J. Walker centered the perspective of working-class black women. We can see this point of view articulated explicitly in her follow-up addresses to the National Negro Business League. In the late summer of 1913, Madam Walker traveled to Philadelphia to attend the annual convention of Booker T. Washington's NNBL. This year, Madam Walker didn't need to force her way to the floor. Unlike the 1912 convention, Walker now found her name listed on the official program alongside black male entrepreneurs offering presentations like "Combining the Real Estate Business with Undertaking" and "Growing and Marketing Watermelons and Cantaloupes" and "Our Experience and Success in the Grocery Business." Madam Walker was slated to give a presentation entitled "Manufacturing Hair Preparations" to those assembled, but her talk gave those present more than an overview of her take on best practices for success in the beauty industry. As Madam Walker shared her accomplishments over the past year, she reminded her audience that she had predicted how much her business would grow; she anticipated even greater success in the future. Moreover, Madam Walker offered insight into how much she continued to prioritize the needs of working-class black women. In keeping with her refusal to consider formal education or elite social status to be the bar for respectability, Madam Walker proclaimed, "I am not ashamed of my past; I am not ashamed of my humble beginning." Well aware of the fact that her comments would circulate far beyond the NNBL meeting hall, she advised all those who might hear about her speech to remember, "Don't think because you have to go down in the wash-tub that you are any less a lady!" Additionally, Madam Walker offered those present further insight into her political perspective and personal sense of self. She explained that through her business, she employed countless African American women, making it possible for them to leave domestic service and maintain a measure of independence from whites. And she concluded by exclaiming that she had entered the business world not for herself alone, but for the good of the entire race. She reiterated this point of view when she returned to the NNBL meeting in 1914. Once again, she spoke about providing jobs for African American women, framing this as her way to help the race. At the conclusion of her address, the NNBL passed a resolution endorsing Madam Walker as the "foremost businesswoman of our race."

Madam Walker's decision to spend a portion of her address describing her commitment to the well-being of her sisters of African descent is not inconsequential. It signaled her perspective on and respect for black women's labor. Madam Walker's business model—employing a traveling sales force of thousands of young black women—offered working-class African American women a form of independent, safe employment and an opportunity to become community-oriented entrepreneurs. As early as 1910, Madam Walker announced "Agents Wanted Everywhere" in her advertisements. And over the course of the decade, she made certain to characterize what it meant to be a Walker agent in terms that would have been especially appealing to working-class black women. Official company documents explained to would-be agents that no barriers prevented them from prospering in the beauty industry. Irrespective of "age, family tree," or "professional connection" any woman "whose ambition leads them to study" and "prepare themselves properly" had the opportunity "to succeed" in this "new day profession." Moreover, Madam Walker's own life experiences demonstrated that working as a beauty culturist offered a path to financial stability, independence, and freedom from white oversight. That Madam Walker had herself spent much of her life as a domestic worker connected her with poor and working-class black women across the country. Using her "washtub to the boardroom" story as an example at every lecture she gave, Madam Walker embodied modern black femininity and community-oriented advancement.

Of course, Madam Walker was not the only black woman who expressed an interest in helping working-class black women at the turn of the twentieth century. Black clubwomen made this commitment a centerpiece of their activism. This directive lay behind the National Association of Colored Women's motto, "Lifting as We Climb." At the same time, however, black reformers and clubwomen could sometimes take an elitist stance and speak in ways that set themselves apart from migrant women or other poor and working-class black women. Despite their progressive political objectives, NACW leaders like Mary Church Terrell could be found opining on occasion that "colored women of education and culture" deplored it when "the dominant race insist[ed] upon gauging the Negro's worth by his most illiterate and vicious representatives." They hoped that elite black women might counteract this tendency by acting as "evidence of the moral, mental, and material progress made by people of color." This elitist perspective certainly reflected NACW members' anxieties about their own status as women who, irrespective of their excellent manners, education, and accomplishments, remained marginalized and discriminated against in the United States. At the same time, these concerns could lead elite and middle-class black reformers to offer advice that could just as easily be read and received as condescending by those working-class and poor black women they hoped to reform. Given this context, it is important to keep in mind that it was not just that Madam Walker talked about helping other black American women but rather *how* she discussed helping other black women that made her a modern race woman.

Madam Walker tended not to speak about working-class, poor, or migrant black women as if they needed to be "improved," "elevated," or "uplifted." Rather, she reached out to them as she traveled across the country, engaging with them as if they were sisters grappling with many of the same life challenges she once experienced. Madam Walker's hands-on approach to meeting with and communicating with agents allowed her to maintain her close identification with the women who demonstrated her method and sold her preparations in towns and cities across the country. This undoubtedly facilitated Madam Walker's ability to recruit a cadre of dedicated agents.

With so few opportunities to work outside of domestic service, work as a Walker agent must have looked like an incredible opportunity to poor and working-class black women. Black domestic workers, for example, continued to average a daily wage of one or two dollars. A Walker agent, however, appeared to have boundless financial opportunities. Given the informality of the business—most agents continued to provide their services in kitchens, parlors, and yards and kept no records of their earnings—it is impossible to quantify an average wage for Walker agents. Walker Manufacturing Company promotional materials, however, promised that an enterprising hairdresser could earn "from three to five dollars a day." Whether or not an agent earned such a sum, all agents had the advantage of choosing their own work hours and organizing appointments around the needs of their families. This type of flexibility attracted a range of women to the business of hair care, including those middle-class and aspiring black women who might once have not considered entering this line of work. Many of these women studied the Walker method and began styling the hair of their friends and neighbors on a part-time basis.

Madam Walker also made certain to keep training programs accessible for a range of black women. It cost twenty-five dollars to complete the course of study and become an agent. Given the potential financial rewards, this would have seemed like a reasonable investment for those who decided to take the plunge. Madam Walker facilitated this in sometimes surprising ways. While traveling in Georgia in 1916, she found the black population to be so impoverished that women couldn't afford the twenty-five-dollar fee to take her course and earn a Walker diploma. She informed her business manager F. B. Ransom that she had reduced the fee to ten dollars and put her new crop of would-be agents on the honor system, telling them "to pay whenever they can and as soon as they pay it all, we'll give them their contract." This was both a smart business calculation (more agents meant more Walker products would be sold) and a demonstration of Madam Walker's commitment to expanding employment options for black women across the country.

Working together, Madam Walker and her agents crafted a more demo-cratic ideal of respectability that extended beyond the educated, the elite, and the reformers of the era. This is apparent in the Walker Manufacturing Company's "Hints to Agents." The "Hints" began telling agents that "Madam Walker is very desirous for all of her agents to make good," in other words, that her concern was that they do their best work and make a sale. The very first hint urged agents to "keep yourself clean as well as your parlor or room in which you do your work. . . . Open your windows—Air it well—When the room is not in use even in winter, throw up the windows, it will drive out the germs." Other hints outlined the business practices that one would expect to find in the best salons: "Keep a waste basket in your parlor and after each customer clean up the hair and matches from the floor." She also urged them to "cleanse and sterilize comb and sponge after each customer." She urged the agents to be attentive to their own breath, teeth, hair, and nails as they worked with their clients. And in the event that they encountered a client whose "breath is offensive," rather than looking down on her, agents were urged to offer her a mint after taking one themselves. Finally, Madam Walker urged agents not to "be narrow and selfish to the extent that you would not sell goods to anyone because they do not take the treatments from you." A sale is a sale, after all. But more importantly, "we are anxious to help all humanity, the poor as well as the rich, especially those of our race. There are thousands who would buy and use the goods who are not able to pay the extra cost of having it done for them. The hair may not grow as rapidly nor look as beautiful, but they will get results, as long as they are satisfied and you have made your profit from the sale, all is well." Rather than condescending to agents, Madam Walker's "Hints" professionalized their work, and in the process made it possible for black customers, no matter how rural their locale, to experience modern hair-care practices.

In addition to blending a humanitarian and political sensibility with prac-tical advice on how to best present oneself and secure a sale, Madam Walker took steps to unify her agents by creating an official organizational body. In early April 1916, Madam Walker floated the idea of organizing her agents into a club past Ransom, asking him, "What do you think about having a National organization of the agents?" She followed up a week later to clarify, "I didn't mean to organize as a Fraternal Society, I meant to organize clubs all over the country, and at some time call a meeting of all the agents and form a National which would be similar to the Women's Federated clubs," in other words, similar to the state federations of the NACW. Ultimately, Madam Walker did organize the agents into local and state clubs: Madam C. J. Walker Hair Culturists Union of America. Together as part of an organized body, they linked labor, style, and politics. In 1917, two hundred Walker agents met in Philadelphia for the first Madam C. J. Walker Hair Culturists Union of America convention. There, Madam Walker offered those assembled an address on "Women's Duty to Women." The agents would take Madam Walker's message to heart, inaugurating a new phase in the history of black women's activism. In the coming decades, the spaces black hairdressers would create, whether in homes or storefront salons, would become essential centers of black communities and incubators of the twentieth-century civil rights movement.

In addition to prioritizing the needs of her agents, Madam Walker took steps to formalize training in black beauty culture. As part of this effort, she worked to institutionalize a curriculum for the Walker Manufacturing Company's system of products. She began by creating a training school, named Lelia College in honor of her daughter, Lelia Walker Robinson. The first Lelia College opened in Pittsburgh. Another would soon open in New York City.

Madam Walker also lobbied to get the Walker method included in the curriculum of black colleges and universities. She had much success in this endeavor during the last half of the decade. Scholars have noted that Madam Walker's effort to institutionalize the Walker system across black colleges in the United States served important practical terms for the success of her business. Such a move created a pipeline of new agents who could sell Walker products and, in turn, reduce the need for Madam Walker herself to travel so extensively. Moreover, the support of black college presidents served as the type of endorsement that would elevate Madam Walker's product line above the competition. Finally, they note that this kind of endorsement added further respectability to the profession of hairdressing. Madam Walker repeatedly insisted that beauty culture was a respectable "means of livelihood," worthy of being taught in schools "as an industry." Every school or college that agreed to teach the Walker system strengthened this emerging understanding of beauty culture as respectable. In letters to school administrators, Madam Walker confidently explained that "we believe the proper care of the scalp and hair adds much to the personal appearance of the individual, and is as necessary as the training of the mind and development of the body." Who could dispute that?

In addition to enhancing the reputation of beauty culture in the eyes of African American reformers, incorporating the Walker system into the curriculum of black colleges and universities broadened the conventional boundaries of "respectable" black women's labor and democratized black beauty culture itself. By 1917, African American women had three ways of learning the Walker method: They could attend Lelia College; they could learn the method as part of a course of study while enrolled in African American colleges such as Tuskegee Institute, Roger Williams University in Tennessee, Wylie College, Mound Bayou Industrial College, or the Daytona Educational and Industrial Training Institute; or they could order the course and learn the Walker method of manicuring, scalp massaging, cleansing and pressing the hair from local agents in their neighborhood, women who took seriously their role in training aspiring beauty culturists and awarding them their diploma upon completion of the course. The diversity of these routes ensured that black women across class and regional lines had access to Madam Walker's course of study. This, in turn, meant that a remarkable array of black women embraced the work of beauty culture. This multifaceted approach to institutionalizing Madam Walker's method ensured that black women's beauty culture remained a truly democratized profession in a highly stratified and hierarchical age. This was a remarkable reimagining of what black women could be and do in the United States.

But by situating her course in black colleges and normal schools, Madam Walker redefined black women's beauty culture in yet another way. Embedding the Walker method in the key black community institutions gave the work—and the Walker brand—a distinctly political edge, and it linked black women's beauty culture to what early twentieth-century black Americans called "black advancement." From the moment of their inception, black colleges had been instrumental to the larger racial uplift agenda at the heart of black associational life and culture. Black colleges, universities, and normal schools served as the training ground for young race men and women. Parents and community members who scrimped and saved and sent their children off to these institutions did so with the expectation that upon graduation, these men and women would go on to serve their communities by creating new institutions and fighting all necessary battles on behalf of the race. The inclusion of the Walker curriculum made modern beauty culture part of this project, supplanting, or at the very least taking a place alongside, long-standing admonitions to embrace the Bible, bath, and broom as an individual and deeply personal political project. As Madam Walker saw it, she, much like black college administrators, engaged in significant political work. Perhaps this is why she signed her letter to Normal Industrial and

Agricultural College by situating herself as a race woman who was as deeply committed to race work as the "gentlemen" in charge of the college. She wished them "a continued success in your great work" and closed by saying, "I am yours for the highest development of the race."

In the latter half of the decade, college presidents moved to add the Walker method to their curricula of their institutions. In exchange for the adoption of her course of study, Madam Walker paid for the construction of a laboratory on the college grounds or took on the cost of training the agent who would oversee the classes. NACW member and college president Mary McLeod Bethune welcomed Madam C. J. Walker's course to Daytona Educational and Industrial Institute. In April 1917, Bethune wrote to Madam Walker and informed her that "for the past four years my girls and myself have been using your wonderful Hair grower. We have proven it to be very beneficial indeed and would be very glad to place it in our school as a *course of study*." Reverend A. M. Townsend, the president of Roger Williams University, also indicated that he welcomed the addition of Madam Walker's course to the school. He wrote, "The idea you have with reference to the placing of your work in institutions for aesthetic training and so on is a proper one and shows that your motive is not a selfish one, but that you are interested in this necessary kind of development for our people." For Townsend, beauty culture—or Madam Walker's form of beauty culture, at least—was an important part of the larger program of racial uplift. He dutifully noted that some of his religious colleagues might disagree. Still, he told her, "we, who have the vision, therefore, will have to stand together in the right and the wisdom of our stand."

Bethune and Townsend's support for Madam Walker's aesthetic project offer insight into the paradigm shift that Madam Walker had set in motion. Both notable African American community leaders and public figures, they enthusiastically associated themselves with Madam Walker. This was not simply an effort on their part to cultivate a wealthy donor; rather, as Bethune's comments suggest, they identified with Madam Walker's aesthetic project. As race women themselves who chose to purchase and utilize Madam Walker's products, Bethune and her students actively claimed Walker's system of hair care in a substantive way, making it part of their own identity. In many respects, this can be understood as an early form of ethical consumer culture. Every time they used the product, Bethune and her students were reminded of Madam Walker's image, her story, and her commitment to the health and advancement of all black Americans. Townsend, meanwhile, associated himself directly with Madam Walker as an institution builder and a leader of the race. For him, the aesthetic project, ostensibly a profoundly personal enterprise, now had important personal significance. By incorporating beauty culture—specifically, training for the Walker method—into black educational institutions, Madam Walker further solidified her status as a race woman. Association with these institutions not only gave Madam Walker, her products, and black beauty culture further legitimacy and respectability, it also aligned Madam Walker with the larger campaign to improve the condition and status of the race. This goal joined black Americans across the political spectrum, and Madam C. J. Walker continued to carve out a place for herself at the center of this movement.

Madam C. J. Walker's political project was also an aesthetic project. And it was an aesthetic project with which a number of African American women were attuned. For despite the warnings of ministers and reformers, young black women were, like their white counterparts in the period, increasingly interested in fashion. Interest in style, as they understood it, was not incompatible with Christian motherhood and domesticity, as male ministers and reformers had long suggested. Nor was a fashionable sensibility a diversion from the political concerns of the day. Fashion, style, and beauty culture were, rather, aspects of modern life that young black women felt they too had a right to enjoy.

We can see this worldview articulated succinctly in *Half-Century* magazine. Named for the fifty years that had elapsed since emancipation, the magazine was owned and edited by a black woman named Katherine Williams. Like Madam Walker, Williams had been a migrant; she migrated from rural Nebraska to Chicago with her parents and understood the mindset of the young black migrant woman. When Williams took charge of *Half-Century* magazine in 1916, she hoped her magazine would appeal to a range of African American women rather than simply members of the black elite. Toward those ends, she planned to "present facts in plain, commonsense language, so that the masses may read and understand." Explaining what African American women could expect to find in the magazine, Williams encouraged those who sought information on the following to subscribe to her magazine:

1. To conduct your home more easily and more cheaply.
2. To dress smartly at the lowest cost.
3. To read the best stories by the leading Colored writers.
4. To bring up and train your children better.
5. To see our own beautiful women depicted in the latest and smartest costumes of Dame Fashion.
6. To know the most novel ideas for entertaining.

7. To be a leader in the social life of your community.
8. To keep in touch with all that is newest and most vital in women's interest, inside and outside the home.

In pieces such as these, Williams succinctly summed up the ways in which interest in beauty and style intersected with community and personal concerns for African American women of her generation. When purchasing and reading her *Half-Century* magazine, readers supported African American writers, learned about issues affecting black women, and read advice on homemaking even as they explored new fashion trends. Moreover, because the magazine used images of black women as models, readers had the opportunity to see beautiful, stylish black women who looked like themselves on the page—a far cry from the grotesque and demeaning representations of servile black women most likely to appear in films and advertisements in the era. In addition to using African American women to model modern fashion, *Half-Century* also advertised the cosmetics sold by the black-owned Overton Hygenic Company.

Like Katherine Williams, Madam C. J. Walker blended the aesthetic, the personal, and the political. Indeed, Madam Walker was uniquely suited to help black women across all social and economic classes fashion themselves into race women of beauty and purpose. Madam Walker promoted a new look—one that had been endorsed by leaders of the black community and one that black women could share irrespective of their class background, level of education, or occupation. Although Madam Walker's lifestyle was certainly out of reach for the overwhelming majority of black women in the United States, her style was hairstyle. Her product was purchasable. Moreover, the opportunity to work as a Walker agent—to become an independent entrepreneur selling beauty and modernity to other black women—may also have served as a way for some to style themselves as modern, twentieth-century black women. Ultimately, by styling themselves after Walker, whether they were agents, customers, or simply admirers of her achievements, black women signaled their own determination to live as modern, twentieth-century women.

This beauty ideal was markedly different from the aesthetic promoted in mainstream advertisements and by the most famous white women celebrities of the period. For fashion inspiration at the turn of the twentieth century, white women turned to advertisements and illustrations featuring the Gibson Girl, a slender, upper-class figure with a mass of curls piled atop her head and a face with childish features. The Gibson Girl served as the national beauty standard for white American women. Then, with the rise of the film industry, a crop of young white actresses emerged to shape American beauty ideals. By the 1910s, stage and film stars like Mary Pickford and Lillian Gish created a new American standard of beauty; fans idolized their long curly blonde tresses, their petite frames, and the chaste young characters they portrayed on screen year after year. White American women looked to famous figures such as these for advice on how to style themselves. This girlishness dominated ideals of American fashion and style despite the achievements of the period's college-educated, accomplished, and politically active New Woman.

Madam Walker and her agents, however, modeled an alternative image of beauty by and for black women. They presented themselves as capable adult women who were also stylish and modern. And as representatives of the Walker Manufacturing Company and all it symbolized, their style and attention to beauty signified that they were women who remained committed to the health and success not only of themselves but of their people.

Younger black women were especially keen to style themselves as modern young women in the middle of the decade, for they were once again on the move. The onset of World War I cut off immigration from Europe to the United States, and black Southerners, looking to escape the poverty and antiblack violence of the South and looking for access to economic opportunity, began moving to urban areas in the North and Midwest in increasing numbers. Between 1914 and 1920, roughly five hundred thousand black Southerners migrated out of the South to the cities of the Northeast and Midwest. These arrivals replaced the flow of unskilled immigrant laborers from Europe, whose movement was curtailed by the outbreak of the war. These black migrants found employment in factories and industrial sites, earning significantly higher wages than they had in the South. Much of this work, however, remained closed to black women, who continued to find their employment options limited to the domestic services. The majority of these migrant women were single women between the ages of thirteen and thirty. As a group, they were young women in search of independence, freedom, and a new life in the city.

The sleek, manageable hair created and modeled by Madam C. J. Walker appealed to this generation of women and soon became the hallmark of black women's style. The hair treatment methods pioneered by Madam Walker and Mrs. Annie Malone signified "the modern way" of styling black women's hair by the end of the decade. Only the most elderly and most traditional women of African descent refused to change their beauty regimens. As one former slave named Mary Williams put it, "I don't think nothin' of this here younger generation." When young women suggested that Williams update her hairstyle, she replied, "I've got along this far without painted jaws and straight hair! And I ain't goin' wear my dresses up to my knees or trail them in the mud, either." Younger black women, however, appreciated this new aesthetic. For them, the headwrap must have not only appeared to be a rural and old-fashioned practice best left in the nineteenth century, but also, more simply, as the styling practice favored by their mothers and grandmothers. For young black women, the prospect of styling their hair in a new and modern way may well have served as a way for them to signify their new status as urban or modern women on the body, or to simply embody their new generational ideal of women's freedom and independence. Given the context of the antiblack visual landscape of the period, we would do well to think of this form of black women's beauty culture as a form of everyday resistance for young black women. By choosing modernity and health, they disrupted the visual landscape. Most importantly, this image of beauty remained attainable for a range of black women. Modern, respectable, and capable, it served as the aesthetic companion to the race woman's political ideology.

This was not the hairdo of a child or a wealthy heiress whose main talent was her ability to enchant men. Rather, this was the look of a race woman, a woman who could stride ahead and take up her burden in the heat of the day. And it was a look that was embraced by a generation of black women who appreciated Madam Walker's aesthetic and political projects. Black women transferred their affinity for the products into respect and admiration for the woman who was the image of the business and brand. Indeed, though she herself never attended one of Madam Walker's addresses in person and despite the fact that she used Malone's Poro system on her clients, the teacher, clubwoman, and part-time hairdresser Mamie Garvin Fields (a self-described modern married woman who was half of a "modern young couple" in 1915) had a strong sense of who Madam Walker was and why she mattered to African Americans. Fields credited Madam Walker for reinventing and expanding the possibilities for black women's style. She recalled:

> Years ago, Negro women didn't straighten their hair. We just used to wash it, brush it out, and arrange it according to the type of hair we had. The type of hair could be any, from African to European and everything in between. Mine was one of those in between. . . . The people with the European type of hair dressed it like the white women around. The people with the African hair wore African styles. They made a lot of little plaits, or they made cornrows. Or else they divided the hair in sections and wrapped them with thread. When that was through, each part stood off like Topsy's hair, in *Uncle Tom's Cabin*. . . .
>
> Anyway, a Madame C. J. Walker made it possible for black women to straighten their hair and then style it whatever way they wanted to. They say that Madame Walker got the idea of straightening hair one day when she was

ironing clothes. . . . When Madame Walker lectured, she said that those inventions came to her "in a dream." She never went to school for this. But, they tell me, that lady really could inspire you with her lectures, because they told how she started from a humble beginning, and everybody there could see how far from that beginning she had come. Then, she had a beautiful face, beautiful hair, dressed elegantly. When she stood up to talk, a go-ahead, up-to-date black woman was talking, and the women listened to what she had to say. Before long, this Negro woman who never went to a beauty school invented the products to go with the equipment she had dreamt. There were the shampoos, the oils to straighten with, the treatments for hair troubles. Then she also created a method, which people flocked to her to study. All of that, put together, was "the Walker System." By selling her system, Madame Walker became a millionaire. Other people copied her. Annie M. Turnbo Malone invented "the Poro System."

Although Fields clearly did not have all the details of Madam Walker's story in order, her description of Madam Walker illustrates just how important a figure she had become by 1915. For Fields and other modern black women of her generation, Walker was "a go-ahead, up-to-date black woman." Madam Walker, in other words, modeled what was possible for a new generation of African American women.

In the process, Madam Walker expanded the limits of the definition of an American New Woman. The moniker New Woman was applied to or claimed by a range of American women at the turn of the twentieth century. For some, the New Woman referred to those women who were gaining access to higher education in greater numbers, moving into the public sphere, and placing their education in the service of political and social reform. Although scholars generally apply the term "New Woman" to white American women who embraced these activities, African American women understood themselves to be part of this promising cultural development. Many members of the NACW, for example, placed their education in the service of the race, penning intellectual treatises such as Anna Julia Cooper's *A Voice from the South*, traveling the world to raise support for the antilynching campaign as Ida B. Wells did, or, as Mary Church Terrell did, giving lectures to international conventions of women to raise awareness about the many obstacles facing women of African descent in the United States. As black women of education and means, however, they considered themselves charged with a special set of responsibilities. They saw themselves as agents able to mobilize their education, femininity, and good sense, using it to move into spaces where black men might be refused entry, and using that ability to create just enough space to build institutions in their communities. Many of these women crafted insightful, thoroughly intellectual defenses of their work, pioneering intersectional critiques of racism and sexism. And they styled themselves as role models for their communities—offering a robust representation of modern black womanhood: They were educated, stylish, politically committed, race-conscious women who were eminently capable of promoting positive change in black communities.

As inspiring and transformative as these women were, Madam Walker offered something more for an even larger demographic of African American women. Madam Walker embodied an image of ideal black womanhood that was accessible to her agents and customers irrespective of education or income. Walker agents were modern black women who tied their approach to community engagement to their sense of themselves as modern. And those black women who purchased Walker products also, as early twentieth-century marketers increasingly understood, bought into the aspirational tale of the product's namesake. By 1916, black women weren't simply purchasing Madam Walker's products or using her techniques. While other advertisements in the period sold an American Dream to consumers, Madam Walker's products came to represent an African American woman's dream. Consuming these products enabled black women across the country to buy into this dream.

Indeed, Madam Walker's "from the washtub to the boardroom" trajectory served as an inspiration to countless young black women. She served as an example confirming that it was possible to make a better life for oneself in the United States. In that sense, she modeled the collective hopes of the Great Migration during World War I. As Mamie Garvin Fields's description of Madam Walker suggests, black women also took pride in the story of Madam Walker's meteoric rise from the cabin to the boardroom and her commitment to the health, well-being, and advancement of black people. Soon, it was not simply Madam Walker's beauty regimen or style that black women sought to copy. It was something more intangible—a Walker ethos, perhaps—that modern women like Fields sought to embody for themselves as they moved further into the twentieth century. To put it another way, by 1916, Madam C. J. Walker had already become an African American icon.

CHAPTER SIX

~

Icon

Around 1916, Madam C. J. Walker decided, once again, to move. This time she chose for herself a site in the bucolic village of Irvington-on-Hudson. A wealthy enclave just north of New York City, Irvington-on-Hudson claimed a number of notable residents from prominent white American families, including scions of industry such as the Rockefellers. It was a prestigious and daring location for any black American to build a home and take up residence. Madam Walker believed that given her status and her means, Irvington-on-Hudson was just the right place for her.

As keenly attuned to the cultural dynamics of the moment as she had been throughout her career, Madam Walker understood that she had once again reached a new phase in her life. With the success of her Madam C. J. Walker Manufacturing Company, her national reputation as a philanthropist, and her role in various politically oriented African American organizations, Madam Walker now had broad name recognition within African American communities across the United States. By 1916, Madam Walker represented something far larger than the sum of her business earnings and activities. The girl named Sarah Breedlove who had been born on the Grand View plantation on the banks of the Mississippi had transformed herself into a celebrity and an icon for black Americans.

What exactly was it that made Madam C. J. Walker a celebrity and an icon? Although it is tempting to think of celebrity status as something that is thrust upon a person, scholars have shown that this is not exactly the case. Celebrities create a public persona that they actively cultivate through conscious choices about self-representation, marketing, and publicity. According to the theorist Nicole Fleetwood, "becoming a celebrity icon is a labor-intensive choice that involves sculpting one's features, developing public recognition, building identification, and turning one's self into a vehicle of desirability and adoration. In essence, the celebrity icon is manufactured and groomed." In other words, "celebrity iconicity is an aspiration, deliberately sought out by those who hope to reach its heights." At the same time, as theorist Sharon Marcus shows, this celebrity status is negotiated with fans and members of the public who attach all kinds of meaning to the name, image, and activities of those celebrities they admire and seek to emulate.

Madam Walker took several steps to deliberately craft a public persona throughout her professional life. She very carefully fashioned herself from Sarah Breedlove into Madam C. J. Walker. She strategically marketed her business and herself to an ever-widening audience. She placed her compelling and wildly successful public persona at the heart of her thriving business empire. And by the middle of the decade, Madam Walker's name and image had become rife with meaning for African Americans who increasingly viewed her as an admirable public figure. Madam Walker continued to carefully craft her public image even as she remained politically active and crisscrossed the country promoting her business. By the end of the decade, black audiences not only admired her, they felt as if they personally knew her.

Additionally, Madam Walker remained at the center of national developments. Her hair-care empire and all that she put into the business to ensure its success dovetailed with the rise of modern, mass-market consumer culture in the United States. Her new Irvington-on-Hudson mansion was to be a residence befitting her new cultural position as a celebrated public figure and a monument to her unparalleled success. By the time Madam Walker took up residence in her new home, a growing number of commentators and consumers both within and outside the United States projected meaning onto Madam Walker's image, name, and life story. They would continue to do so for decades after Madam C. J. Walker's untimely death in 1919.

Madam C. J. Walker's new village was located roughly twenty miles from Harlem, a neighborhood in New York City, which was fast becoming a mecca for people of African descent from all parts of the globe. Located in the borough of Manhattan just north of Central Park, Harlem had not always been an African American neighborhood. From the seventeenth to the late nineteenth centuries, black New Yorkers remained largely concentrated in lower Manhattan neighborhoods dominated by European immigrants. Over the centuries, black American communities worked their way northward in the aftermath of successive antiblack massacres such as the Draft Riots of 1863. By the late nineteenth century, the bulk of the city's black population clustered in the Tenderloin and San Juan Hill neighborhoods on the west side of midtown Manhattan. In the wake of a deadly attack on their neighborhood in 1900, these black Americans too began moving northward in search of a home. This migration accelerated after the pioneering African American realtor Philip A. Payton Jr. began securing leases for black tenants in modern, spacious buildings on 133rd Street in the heart of Harlem. In the earliest years of black migration to the area, African Americans congregated in apartment buildings situated between Eighth Avenue and the Harlem River on the west and east, with southern and northern boundaries from 130th to 145th streets. As older white residents of German descent began fleeing the neighborhood in droves, black real estate investors and black churches purchased neighboring properties and rented them to African American tenants. Black cabarets and churches soon followed, ensuring that the new neighborhood provided cultural sustenance for its inhabitants, whether on Saturday night or on Sunday morning.

Although the precise figures for New York City's black population are difficult to ascertain, it appears that by 1920, about two-thirds of the city's black population resided in Harlem. The neighborhood contained a dynamic mix of people from throughout the diaspora, for by 1917, Harlem had become a destination not just for longtime black residents of the city, but for black migrants from the South and immigrants from the Caribbean and South America. While many of these residents traveled to Harlem in search of economic opportunity and freedom from antiblack racism, others were artists, intellectuals, bohemians, and activists from around the world, all drawn to the most exciting city in the United States. As a result, Harlem emerged as a center of cultural and political life in the African diaspora. As Madam C. J. Walker put it in a 1916 letter to her attorney and business manager F. B. Ransom when explaining her decision to move from Indianapolis to New York: "As regards my coming back to Indianapolis Mr. Ransom that is clear out of the question. . . . There is so much more joy living in New York."

In addition to feeling drawn to this cultural mecca, Madam Walker certainly wanted to remain in close proximity to her daughter, Lelia Walker Robinson, who had relocated to Harlem to oversee the construction and management of Harlem's new Lelia Beauty College, the family-owned salon and beauty training school. Lelia took up residence in an elegant multistory townhouse at 108 136th Street, just around the corner from the first apartments brokered for African Americans by Payton. The neighboring townhouse at 110 West 136th Street was home to Lelia College. As she settled into her new home, Lelia set about making the space the center of Harlem's emerging black arts scene. Within just a few years, Lelia's Dark Tower salon would achieve international renown as a gathering space for the intellectuals and artists of the Harlem Renaissance.

By building her new home in Irvington-on-Hudson, just a short commute from New York City, Madam Walker now found herself both in close proximity to her daughter and in the orbit of the black political and cultural luminaries who regularly gathered and held court in Harlem. Race men and women like W.E.B. Du Bois, along with myriad poets, writers, artists, musicians, and entertainers, were all making a home for themselves in Harlem. Together, these new arrivals were debating and redefining what it meant to be a race man or race woman in the twentieth century. Madam Walker extended the boundaries of this milieu to her home in Irvington-on-Hudson. For in addition to serving as a monument to her successful business, Madam Walker's new home became an expression of her identity and consciousness as a modern race woman. Her palatial new home became a crucial new stage upon which she both constructed, instructed, and performed as one of the leading African American icons at the dawn of American celebrity culture.

In keeping with her commitment to "race work," Madam Walker insisted on hiring an African American architect to design her Irvington-on-Hudson property. She chose Vertner Woodson Tandy, a young architect well on his way to a long and distinguished career. Originally from Kentucky, Tandy attended Tuskegee Institute in Alabama and went on to study architecture at Cornell University in New York, ultimately becoming the school of architecture's first African American graduate and New York State's first licensed black architect. Tandy solidified his reputation after designing a new neo-Gothic sanctuary for St. Philip's Episcopal Church once the congregation decided to leave the Tenderloin and move uptown to Harlem. Tandy also designed Lelia's Harlem townhouses at 108–110 West 136th Street. Having just completed the renovations on these buildings, Tandy was well acquainted with the Walker women's penchant for beauty and glamour. With that in mind, Tandy set about designing a grand home for the foremost businesswoman of the race. The residence was completed in 1918.

Madam C. J. Walker moved to Irvington-on-Hudson in June of that year. Her new Italianate-style mansion featured a white stucco exterior with a Spanish tile roof and sat on more than four acres on the Hudson River in Westchester County, not too far from the home of John D. Rockefeller and the estates of other captains of industry. The twenty-room, twenty-thousand-square-foot home offered commanding views of the Hudson River and

Palisades, and, according to the *New York Times* and Walker Manufacturing Company press releases, cost $250,000 (approximately $4.5 million in 2019) to build.

An estate so elegant with a view so grand deserved a name. And Madam Walker's home soon had one: Villa Lewaro. According to family lore, world-famous tenor Enrico Caruso—a friend of Lelia Walker Robinson—visited the home and suggested that they combine the first two letters of Lelia's name (LeWaRo) to form the name of the estate. Madam Walker agreed.

Villa Lewaro, with its tapestries, sculptures, library, music room, and gardens, served as more than an elegant retreat for Madam Walker. It signaled to all observers that Madam Walker was indeed the foremost businesswoman of her race, an innovator who had earned her place in this exclusive enclave. And although some observers—both black and white—might have found cause to bristle at the idea of a black woman purchasing such an imposing estate, Madam Walker insisted that her home was not a frivolous example of conspicuous consumption. She insisted that her home should be understood as a "Negro institution," an example of the "business possibilities within the race" and a symbol "of what a lone woman accomplished." She hoped that Villa Lewaro would serve as a source of inspiration to young black Americans.

With this in mind, Madam Walker made sure that her home remained open to guests and visitors. Indeed, she ensured that her parties served as important spaces to showcase emerging black talent. But the home also served another function. It was a center of black entertainment and the arts. On the eve of the Harlem Renaissance, Madam Walker began modeling what it meant to support black artists. Although she first began cultivating this habit in Indianapolis, Madam Walker found that with a space like Villa Lewaro and its proximity to New York City, her ability to enjoy, showcase, and, in the process, promote black artists expanded exponentially. In the coming months, Madam Walker used her elegant parties and soirees as occasions to promote the work of African American writers and musicians like poet Paul Laurence Dunbar and early jazz pioneer James Reese Europe. In doing so, she became a cultivator and disseminator of emerging African American art and cultural forms. These events often received coverage in the black press, which now recounted Madam Walker's moves breathlessly.

Soon, Madam Walker began using an image of Villa Lewaro on promotional materials. Ever intuitive about the relationship between her personal presentation and the success of her company, Madam Walker understood that her home also served as an extension of her business enterprise and the Walker brand. The home would appear in later advertisements alongside a photo of Madam Walker, symbolizing Villa Lewaro's centrality to her public persona and her brand. These advertisements fused Madam Walker's extraordinary tale of self-fashioning with the image of her "palatial home," making Villa Lewaro—both in name and in image—a metonym for Madam C. J. Walker. Just as the image of the White House calls to mind the president of the United States, depictions of Villa Lewaro conjured up Madam C. J. Walker and her "washtub to the boardroom" personal narrative. The building's recognizability among the black American populace, the vast majority of whom had never and would never see Villa Lewaro in person, further signaled Madam Walker's elevation to an icon.

As the decision to incorporate Villa Lewaro into advertising campaigns for the Walker Manufacturing Company suggests, Madam C. J. Walker understood the power of publicity. She had an astute awareness of emerging American advertising techniques and operated on its cutting edge. And throughout her career, Madam Walker continued to carefully craft and control the dissemination of her image. Handwritten addenda to press releases by her company indicate just how involved she was in every sentence used to construct her public persona and market the products of the Madam C. J. Walker Manufacturing Company. Her attention to her public image began with the way she first framed her skills in her earliest years as a beauty culturist—as a hair *grower* rather than a hair *straightener*—and continued as she became a nationally renowned businesswoman. Throughout these years, the essential pieces of Madam Walker's origin story remained unchanged. She continued to emphasize the importance of health and good hygiene, and she centered herself within black cultural traditions. By framing her story this way, Madam Walker tapped into a history of African healing that not only lay at the heart of the experiences of her early life, but also would have served as reminders of a rural past, which might, for migrants to cities across the country, sometimes be nostalgic. This story continued to give Madam Walker a kind of grounded authenticity and a clear connection to her roots as a Southern black woman who was the daughter of slaves, despite her current wealth and fame. It was also a tale of divine inspiration, one that Madam Walker characterized as her unique and special gift to the world. That she followed all of this up with a demonstrated record of support for black institutions and causes ensured that she maintained the respect of people of African descent in the United States. At a moment when manufacturers were learning how to advertise the American Dream to consumers, Madam Walker consciously embodied an African American dream for black women. And Madam Walker's business provided consumers with the tools and know-how to refashion their appearance and participate in a dramatically growing national beauty culture that built community and promised liberatory pleasure.

Madam Walker cultivated her public image and rose to fame at a pivotal time in the United States, for this was the moment when the nation experienced the emergence of modern celebrity culture. Although several individuals had achieved levels of fame in the preceding centuries, the turn of the twentieth century saw a heightened mass interest in the activities of public figures—especially those individuals who built careers within entertainment industries, beauty culture, and leisure culture. Urbanization, increased access to forms of public amusement and entertainment, the expansion of media platforms, and a growing obsession with consumer culture created a climate where Americans across racial and class lines self-identified as "fans" of a new crop of famous figures. In this context, stars of stage, sports, and screen stepped into the role once occupied by ministers, generals, and political figures in the United States; celebrities now served as admirable figures for the public. By the early twentieth century, celebrities played an essential role in shaping the goals, aspirations, and desires of people across the country. As fans, meanwhile, Americans developed an appetite for learning all they could about the exciting exploits and the mundane daily habits of those public figures they admired. In addition to consuming as much information as they could, some fans sought a closer connection with popular figures.

Although scholars tend to focus on the famous white individuals who manufactured modern celebrity culture, it is worth remembering that savvy African Americans like Madam C. J. Walker also tapped into these cultural phenomena as they built their own public personas. By 1916, Madam Walker had emerged as one of the first twentieth-century black celebrities, succeeding nineteenth-century political luminaries like Frederick Douglass and anticipating the African American artists and entertainers who would burst onto the international scene during the Harlem Renaissance. Indeed, African Americans approached and understood Madam Walker in terms scholars usually attribute to white celebrities. One African American publicist wrote to Madam Walker later that year offering to represent her on her next tour. Addressing the letter to "Mme. C. J. Walker, America's Miracle Worker," R. G. Doggett let Madam Walker know that he had a vision for revamping her already popular lectures. He proposed a joint tour with Madam Walker's friend and acquaintance Sissieretta Jones, the "Black Patti." He envisioned a "song and lecture tour with you beginning the first of the year or just as soon as you are ready." And with the assurance and a bit of calculated flattery appropriate for a publicist, he noted, "I am certain that with your brilliant lecture and this great singer and with the way I have planned my publicity campaign our tour will be the prime sensation of the year. I am sure we will turn people away at every engagement. For are not Mme. C. J. Walker and Mme. S. Jones two of America's greatest women?" Noting that he had heard that this was expected to be Madam Walker's "farewell lecture tour" he declared, "I am willing to give up all of my plans for the present and devote my entire energies to the making of the balance of your tour the most memorable in the history of the race. I can do this because it is the work I love best to do."

Doggett wasn't the only one who hoped to cash in on the growing interest in Madam Walker's story. The black press also publicized Madam Walker's activities. Articles in African American newspapers such as the *Chicago Defender*, the *Indianapolis Freeman*, and the *Pittsburgh Courier* continued to publish articles on Madam Walker's business, her life story, and her "splendid" home, Villa Lewaro. But by 1917, it was not only the black press that expressed interest in Madam Walker. Indeed, white-owned newspapers published for white readers also covered Madam Walker's activities. In the process, they contributed to the expansion of Madam C. J. Walker's fame.

In 1917, as Villa Lewaro was nearing completion, the *New York Times* published a short profile on Madam Walker. Given the fact that the paper was not known to be especially fair or decent toward subjects of African descent (mainstream press coverage of African Americans often included racially coded language or denigrating remarks about people of African descent in this period), the relatively straightforward nature of the piece is surprising. Although the piece didn't capitalize the N in "Negro"—a journalistic choice widely understood as rude to African Americans—the piece did refer to Madam Walker simply as "Mrs. Sarah J. Walker . . . or Mme. Walker, as she is more generally known." With the breathless, gossipy tone newly in vogue in the period, the profile began by noting, "They say she has a cool million, or nearly that." Precipitated by her move to Irvington-on-Hudson, the bulk of the article focused on the design of the mansion and the "puzzled" and "surprised" reactions of the wealthy white residents of the village. But the article also offered an overview of Madam Walker's business and her rise to prominence. It emphasized her hard work and "perseverance," and quoted her saying, "When, a little more than twelve years ago, I was a washerwoman, I was considered a good washerwoman and laundress. I am proud of that fact. At times I also did cooking, but, work as I would, I seldom could make more than $1.50 a day. I got my start by giving myself a start. It is often the best way. I believe in push, and we must push ourselves." With much of the profile framed in this way, the *New York Times* painted Madam

C. J. Walker in terms quite familiar to white readers. In their hands, Madam Walker appeared to be a black version of the popular Horatio Alger figure, a person who had achieved an enviable version of the American Dream and "an Estate at Irvington, Overlooking Hudson and Containing All the Attractions That a Big Fortune Commands," simply by hard work, pluck, and good luck.

Even contemptuous profiles of Madam Walker exhibited the kind of awe-struck tone generally associated with the coverage of celebrities. The *Literary Digest*, for example, barely contained its mixture of scorn and awe when describing Madam Walker. "Fourteen years ago Mrs. Walker was earning her living at the washtub. To-day she is the richest negress in New York," the piece began. Not content merely to use the term "negress," which most black American women found repugnant, the piece continued by placing "Madam" and "beauty parlors" in scare quotes, a journalistic move that emphasized the author's skepticism about the whole enterprise. Still, the author could not argue with the fact of Madam Walker's achievement: "Her present home, with its artistic furnishings, is worth more than $50,000, and—altho her neighbors-to-be are not yet aware of it—she is building a mansion in an exclusive residence section up the Hudson which it is estimated will cost close to a quarter of a million. And 'Madam' Walker made all her money through the vanity of her colored sisters!"

A much more respectful profile ran in the *Kansas City Star*. Written by Frances L. Garside, a white woman journalist whose career included several profiles on successful American businesswomen, the piece described Garside's impressions of Madam Walker in great detail. After arriving for her appointment, she wrote, "I was taken up-stairs and seated in the drawing-room to await madam's convenience. I am not a Southerner; I waited." Garside continued:

> When she came into the room a few minutes later I realized how adaptable my sex is to change from poverty to wealth, for Mrs. Walker, washerwoman fourteen years ago, carried her generous weight gracefully on high French heels and wore an expensive pink-flowered lavender silk dressing-gown on a weekday morning, with a lack of self-consciousness few of us know when we get on our Sunday clothes. She has an income of one-quarter of a million dollars a year. She made every cent of her money without aid or encouragement from any living soul. Pause while you take off your hat to her.

In addition to describing Madam Walker's now-famous rise from obscurity and her philanthropic donations, the piece highlighted her home furnishings and praised her excellent taste. It did so in terms designed to elicit admiration rather than envy or resentment from readers:

> There is one of those big $200 Victrola in the bedroom hall, and I thought one would surely satisfy, but I saw another in the drawing-room covered with gold leaf to match a gold-leafed grand piano, and an immense gold-leafed harp. That isn't all, oh, you who are buying a $25 graphophone on the instalment plan and satisfying the cravings of your soul for music at the ten-cent store! In the main hall there is a player-organ that reaches to the ceiling!

Finally, Garside commended Madam Walker for her character and philanthropy. She noted admirably, "Madam Walker is the only negro woman on earth who ever gave $1,000 to the Y.M.C.A., and she maintains, year after year, six students at Tuskegee, Ala., paying all their expenses. She lives in luxury, but is not a profligate, giving to the poor what many white folks of her income devote to riotous living." Garside's point of view was clear. Irrespective of race, Madam C. J. Walker was an unqualified success, someone all the readers of the Kansas City newspaper could and should admire.

For African American readers, and black women readers in particular, items such as these represented more than mere coverage of Madam Walker's taste, status, and success. Rather, turn-of-the-century black Americans would have read these stories in light of their awareness of the Jim Crow context in which they lived, an era when examples of African American success could easily generate a violent backlash from white observers. As historian Leon Litwack has noted, "When whites took to the streets, as in Wilmington, North Carolina, in 1898, and in Atlanta, Georgia, in 1906 . . . the principal targets were blacks 'out of their place,' and invariably these included leading and propertied blacks." For example, in Atlanta in 1906, a mob of ten thousand whites, whipped into a frenzy over false rumors of black men assaulting white women, spent four days and nights attacking black residents of the city. Their principal targets appeared to be the most successful African Americans, those with property and education who lived in the city's established black middle-class neighborhoods. Fifteen years later, in response to the economic success of the black business corridor of Tulsa, Oklahoma (known at the time as Black Wall Street), an armed white mob, with the active support of law enforcement and local authorities, descended upon African Americans, driving the black population from the city from the city. In this context, descriptions of Walker's mansion and belongings represented far more than her wealth; they symbolized forms of liberation to which countless black Americans aspired and evidence of black achievement that white Americans found objectionable.

This symbolism certainly shaped reactions to press coverage of Madam Walker's automobiles. In a moment where reformers had only just gotten used to the idea of women riding bicycles, Madam C. J. Walker owned (and drove) her own automobiles and employed a chauffeur, taking them with her as she toured the nation and the Caribbean. In the process, Madam Walker embodied a modern spirit of mobility in vogue with early twentieth-century black women. Moreover, she did this in the face of white Americans who perceived black automobile ownership to be a threat to white supremacy. In 1917, the *New York Times* dutifully noted that "Mme. Walker maintains four automobiles." That same year, a newspaper in Macon, Georgia, "reported at least four incidents in which black owners of automobiles were beaten and warned to dispose of their vehicles." For example, when "Henry Watson, a prosperous black farmer in Georgia, acquired a car and drove with his daughter into the nearest town," the "local residents forced them at gunpoint to get out of the car, poured gasoline on it, and set it on fire [and] insulted Watson's daughter." In Abbeville, South Carolina, "a mob confronted Mark Smith, a black resident, while he was driving his car with his wife, mother, and children. The mob blocked the road and shot Smith repeatedly as he tried to escape." One black Abbeville resident summed up the situation saying, "lookes as if they dont want to see the colored people advance or progress to eny extent." It was in this context that members of the public, both black and white, received and made meaning out of coverage of Madam Walker's patterns of consumption.

Aware of the interest in her life story and attuned to the nation's growing interest in visual culture, Madam Walker incorporated the stereopticon into her lectures. With each public address, Madam Walker now included images of her Indianapolis factory and Villa Lewaro. In doing so, she accelerated a process where images of her home and factory functioned as metonyms that called to mind Madam C. J. Walker's name, her products, her politics, her wealth, and her remarkable life story. Madam Walker's constant crisscrossing the country to give her lectures and sell her products enabled a range of African American women to see her face-to-face. That she made these trips so often on her own, driving her own car, was not inconsequential. To black women who looked up to Madam Walker, these trips and lectures offered tangible evidence of the control Madam Walker seemed to have over her own life and destiny.

Madam C. J. Walker's unique position in the United States made others want to tell her story. Indeed, there was talk of a movie about her life. On April 18, 1918, Charles Allmon of St. Louis wrote to Madam Walker to follow up on an earlier conversation they had had about recruiting agents, creating stereopticon slides, and "making moving pictures of your home on the Hudson, including your factories and other places in Indiana." Allmon now suggested that Madam Walker consider allowing him to write, stage, and produce a movie called *The Life of Madam Walker*, with Madam Walker herself, "of course" taking the leading role in the picture. "The advantage of having such a picture will be," he explained, "that you can book it at all the race theaters at a handsome rate." For his part, Allmon was so excited about the idea that he had already begun work on the screenplay. At some point, a movie does seem to have been completed, for in a January 1918 letter to her business manager, F. B. Ransom—months, in fact, before the inquiry from Allmon—Walker mentioned in passing: "I wish the picture would come. I would like very much to see it. Do you think it serves as much of an ad for the business? Does it end with the prayer that was suggested?"

Others contacted the Madam Walker Manufacturing Company inquiring about writing Madam Walker's biography. I. Johnson, the principal of the "Colored Public School" of Indianapolis, wrote to Madam Walker in early January 1918 to inform her that he was "engaged in the writing of a history of Indiana Colored People" and intended to include her in his chapter on "men and women of high attainment." As he saw it, Madam Walker remained a representative of Indiana despite her relocation to New York. He wrote, "The fact that you are not now living in the state will not in any way interfere with your having recognition in my history." And he respectfully concluded his letter with a request: "Will you be kind enough to let me know when you will again be in Indianapolis that I may have an interview with you to get a sketch of your life? A personal interview is important." Similarly, in March of that year, a representative from the Inter-State Sales and Advertising Agency wrote with what they "regard[ed] as a most capital idea, namely, the compilation of a biography of your life, in book form." As the writer (who didn't sign the letter) saw it, there were three reasons Madam Walker should allow them to undertake this endeavor: "First, from a business point of view, it is profitable inasmuch as it is a most effective method of advertising ones' personality and business." Given her keen marketing instincts, Madam Walker would surely have understood his point. The writer then appealed to Madam Walker's consciousness as a race woman: "Second, from a race point of view, it will serve to stimulate Negro men and women, who possess talent and ability to initiate enterprises in the commercial field." Like Madam Walker, the writer believed "that those persons of our race who have achieved success and distinction in public life, have a solemn obligation to present to the present and future generations, the methods adopted and the obstacles and difficulties encountered in securing position, prestige and power in the business, scientific, and political field." Finally, the writer asserted the "value" of biography as a form, adding that "I plan to place it in the public libraries, and in the various libraries of Negro schools and colleges." Coverage like this extended Madam Walker's name recognition and celebrity status beyond African American circles. Few other African Americans in the era could make such a claim. And those who did, say, heavyweight champion Jack Johnson, hardly received the favorable coverage that Madam Walker received. Indeed, some white Americans responded positively to coverage about Madam Walker's life:

Rocky Ford, Colorado December 10, 1919,
Mrs. Sarah J. Walker

I am writing you from admiration and astonishment of your success in gaining the wealth you have, not many have the brains to do this without financial help, and you did it all this without [illegible] to start on, how I would love to see your lively place and see you enjoying it while this privilege will never be mine I can imagine how fine it would feel to have every desire fulfilled. I am sure you will be able to help others help themselves in giving them work and advice. I am a white woman but my husband fought to protect your race and I was taught from a child to respect the colored race, I take this method to congratulate you.

Wishing you a Merry Christmas and Happy New Year.

Very Truly,
Mrs. H. M. Minos

As this letter suggests, those whites who responded positively to Madam Walker viewed her as an excellent representative of African American achievement: a black "first." Black firsts often become iconic figures as they broke new ground and overcome obstacles. Mrs. Minos, for example, admires Madam Walker both because of the extraordinary success she has garnered and because Madam Walker has managed to achieve so much as a black woman. This type of admiration makes it so that black Americans often become, as the cultural critic Nicole Fleetwood explains, a different kind of celebrity in the United States: They achieve the status of racial icons. This type of admiration, as Fleetwood notes, often contains—whether intentional or not—an implicit indictment of the rest of the black population for failing to live up to the extraordinary standard set by someone like Madam Walker. In other words, twentieth-century black icons were often considered by white Americans to be exceptions that proved the rule of the inherent goodness of American capitalism and democracy and the innate deficiency of the majority of African Americans. And for those whites who would hear her story, Madam Walker might be considered a rare example of African American achievement.

Madam Walker was well aware of this emerging celebrity culture. In fact, as her careful marketing and advertising efforts make clear, she was a cocreator of it. Madam C. J. Walker not only tapped into an emerging discourse and used it to shape her persona but also, in the process, helped to define it.

Documents in the archive suggest that Madam C. J. Walker did not especially concern herself with what white Americans thought. Instead, she placed her celebrity in the service of the race, continuing to support the political agendas most important to African Americans in the period. Madam Walker joined the Executive Committee of the New York NAACP. She continued to attend the NNBL convention. She also remained involved with NACW initiatives, attending the 1918 biennial NACW convention in Denver. And she maintained a friendship with the beauty culturist and community activist Lucille Randolph (who used the Walker system on her clients) and her husband A. Philip Randolph. A socialist union organizer and civil rights activist, A. Philip Randolph founded the radical black newspaper *The Messenger* in 1917 and would go on to found the Brotherhood of Sleeping Car Porters, a labor union for black railroad Pullman porters, in 1925. Advertisements for Walker Manufacturing Company products would be among the first in *The Messenger*.

Madam Walker also expanded her efforts to protect the business interests of African Americans. In 1918, Walker invited black manufacturers of beauty products to Villa Lewaro, engaging them in a discussion about how they might best protect their business interests. Just as "Banker, Wholesale and Retail merchants" created associations to protect their trades, presumably coming to agreements about prices and practices, Madam Walker and other black manufacturers hoped to establish some principles and guidelines upon which they could all agree. They organized themselves into National Negro Cosmetic Manufacturer's Association (NNCMA) on the grounds that they shared an interest not just in their business, but in the greater good of people of African descent. Noting the emergence of new, non-black-owned beauty companies targeting black women consumers, the NNCMA explained that "the white man who is not interested in Colored Women's Beauty only looks to further his own gains and put on the market Preparations that are absolutely of no aid whatsoever to the Skin, Scalp, or Hair." Unlike business such as these, the black-owned companies of the NNCMA made sure to publicly proclaim that they had the best interest of black women in mind when they created their beauty products.

Madam Walker also advocated for an end to antiblack racism, lynching, and mob attacks on black neighborhoods. This campaign required a great deal of attention from black activists, for these were years fraught with anti-black violence. In response, Madam Walker remained vocal in her denunciation of these incidents. The 1917 East St. Louis Masscare was one especially stark example. During the first week of July, well over one thousand whites descended upon black residents in the city of East St. Louis, Illinois. The mob attacked men, women, and children on streetcars, chased families, and set fires to homes, all under the protective gaze of the local police and the National Guard. By the time the massacre came to an end, more than one hundred black Americans lay dead. Thousands of black refugees, meanwhile, left their property behind as they fled across the Mississippi River to St. Louis, Missouri.

Along with other black activists across the country, Madam Walker recommitted herself to the fight against racism in the wake of the East St. Louis Massacre. According to a synopsis of the 1917 National Convention of Walker Agents, Madam Walker gave an address urging her audience to take up the fight for justice and a more perfect union. "We must not let our love of our country, our patriotic loyalty," she proclaimed, "cause us to abate one whit in our protest against wrong and injustice. We should protest until the American sense of justice is so aroused that such affairs as the East St. Louis Riot be forever impossible." The Walker agents attending the convention agreed. The agents sent a formal expression of protest to President Woodrow Wilson. They saw themselves not just as hair culturists but, as they put it, women who wrote "in a larger sense representing the twelve million Negroes" who "have keenly felt the injustice done our race and country through the . . . horrible race riot at East St. Louis." They reminded the president of the loyalty and patriotism of the nation's black citizens, and then "respectfully submit[ted] to you this our protest against the continuation of such wrongs and injustice in this land of the free and home of the brave, and we further respectfully urge that you as President of these United States use your great influence that Congress enact the necessary laws to prevent a recurrence of such disgraceful affairs."

Madam Walker remained especially active in the antilynching movement. In 1917 she joined a delegation of Harlem elites who traveled to the

White House to present a petition calling for antilynching legislation. She mentioned her effort to sway President Wilson in a brief letter to Ransom on August 2, 1917: "I had the honor to be one of the delegates to call at the White House to have audience with the President. He did not see us, but Mr. Tumulty, Mr. Wilson's Secretary received us very kindly and gave us some encouragement. We are now planning a trip to Oyster Bay to see Mr. Roosevelt. Perhaps we shall go this afternoon." In September 1917, Madam Walker joined two hundred delegates attending the radical black activist Monroe Trotter's National Equal Rights League meeting. The attendees voted to denounce the segregation and violence sweeping the nation. They also elected Madam C. J. Walker as the organization's vice president at large. In March 1918, Madam Walker signed an antilynching petition along with 118 other activists and politicians. She also contributed to the NAACP's new antilynching fund in 1919. Unable to attend the meeting scheduled for May 5, Walker asked her friend and NACW president Mary Talbert to deliver a $1,000 check to the NAACP on her behalf. That sum was just a portion, Talbert told the activists in the audience, of Madam Walker's $5,000 donation to the NAACP's antilynching campaign.

In addition to fighting against lynching, Madam Walker also furthered an initiative of the NACW by campaigning for equal rights for black soldiers. With the United States now actively involved in World War I, NACW president Mary Talbert urged the women of the NACW to support the war effort through "Red Cross and relief work" and "food production and conservation." Members of the NACW signed petitions requesting "colored Red Cross nurses" for the war. But they did not limit their war work to activities others might consider safely and appropriately feminine. As race women, they also pledged to "be vigilant against every attempt to arouse the spirit of racial injustice" and to make every effort to ensure that every black soldier "will receive the same consideration as other soldiers."

In her own personal war work, Madam Walker remained equally determined to fight for the rights of black men. She visited black troops as she traveled, and she supported the Circle for Negro War Relief. She also hosted black troops before their deployment to the European battlefield. In December 1917, Lelia and Madam Walker opened the Harlem townhouse to host a farewell concert for the men of the 369th "Harlem Hellfighters" of the 93rd Division of the New York National Guard, feting the regiment as they prepared to embark on their journey to the front in France. And a few weeks later in January, Lelia hosted a "military cotillion" for the 92nd Division's black officers.

Madam Walker's sense of diasporic consciousness also led her to support those who sought to form diasporic organizations. She hoped to join black delegates who planned to travel to Paris as part of a National Race Congress scheduled to take place during the Paris Peace Conference after the armistice brought the hostilities of World War I to a conclusion. And in January 1919, Madam Walker opened Villa Lewaro to a group of individuals who hoped to organize an International League of Darker Peoples.

Madam Walker's activism on behalf of black people did not go unnoticed by the federal government. Indeed, the combination of her activism, her business success, and her popularity with black Americans made her, by definition, a subversive figure. Not surprisingly, the federal government soon placed Madam Walker under state surveillance. Her interest in the National Race Congress earned her a spot on the federal government's list of "Negro Subversives." She was even denied a business passport to visit Europe in February 1919.

Madam Walker was not the first black American to receive such treatment by the United States government or to be perceived as a threat by whites. Several of her contemporaries felt the effects of this backlash. White locals responded violently to the young journalist Ida B. Wells's antilynching reporting and forced her out of the city of Memphis. With a price on her head, Wells was unable to return; she relocated to the city of Chicago. The state tried and convicted heavyweight boxing champion Jack Johnson for violating the Mann Act (which made it illegal to transport a woman across state lines for "immoral purposes") when he took a trip with his white wife. Johnson fled the country and remained exiled in Europe for years, only returning to serve his sentence in 1920. Meanwhile, in response to Johnson's demonstrated excellence in the ring, promoters ensured that heavyweight boxing remained a whites-only enterprise for the next two decades. In the 1920s, a young J. Edgar Hoover classified the Jamaican-born black nationalist Marcus Garvey as one of the most dangerous black men in the United States and sent spies to Harlem to surveil his activities. After a relentless federal campaign to infiltrate Garvey's Universal Negro Improvement Association and discredit Garvey's work, the federal government ultimately indicted Garvey for mail fraud and deported him from the country.

As the treatment of these other black Americans makes clear, Madam Walker was one of the early targets of a federal government that sought to curtail any black activism or effort to improve the status and prospects of black people in the United States. At the same time, however, Madam Walker appears to have escaped much of the scrutiny, hostility, and physical violence that white Americans meted out to other notable and successful African Americans at the turn of the twentieth century. Perhaps the white public was unaware of the extent of her activism. Perhaps they considered women's beauty culture to be too frivolous an activity to arouse much concern. Perhaps she simply passed away before a campaign against her could coalesce and gain steam. Whatever the case, Madam C. J. Walker continued to engage in all aspects of her work until the end of the decade.

Madam C. J. Walker's growing name recognition and political significance made black Americans feel as if they personally knew her. And this, in turn, generated an atmosphere where people from around the nation began reaching out to her for money. This was, of course, a double-edged sword. Her wealth and philanthropy were a part of her brand, but the requests for aid could be overwhelming. Madam Walker captured this tension in a letter to Ransom in mid-January 1918. "I laughed heartily over what they said about me in Chicago. I do not mind if they think I am a millionaire as long as they do not beg me for any more money," she quipped.

This phenomenon began during Madam Walker's days in Indianapolis, soon after her well-publicized donation to the city's YMCA fundraising campaign. As she put it in a 1914 letter to Booker T. Washington, people had the idea that she was wealthier than she actually was. She explained, "I am unlike your white friends who have waited until they were rich and then help, but have in proportion to my success I have reached out and am helping others, which may have been a mistake perhaps because I have been mistaken for a rich woman, which has caused scores of demands for help. Many of whom are so pathetic that it has been impossible for me to turn them down."

These requests for financial help and support increased in intensity during the final years of the decade. Individuals and representatives of African American institutions also wrote letters with request for aid with great frequency. In 1917, William Alfred Fountain, the president of Morris Brown University, wrote to ask for $100 "to make some repairs" in the university's laundry. "Any amount will be highly appreciated," he wrote, "and will be a blessing to the young ladies who will attend this school."

Progressive white activists reached out to Madam Walker for help as well. In April 1918, Mary White Ovington, one of the white founding members of the NAACP, wrote to ask if Madam Walker might help fund a "day nursery" in Brooklyn." As "the only colored nursery in the city" the nursery provided a much-needed service for young black working mothers, and it was suffering, "like other philanthropies," due to the war. Within a week, Madam Walker received a request for support from the Reverend Howard J. Chidley of the First Congregational Church of Winchester, Massachusetts. As one of the trustees of the National Training School in Durham, North Carolina, Chid-ley hoped that Walker would support the school's fundraising campaign. Due to the "pressure of war demands," he explained, "we have had difficulty this year in raising money for the current expenses. We are greatly in need of five thousand dollars at this time to catch up with our current indebtedness." Given these circumstances, Chidley noted that "I should greatly appreciate a gift from you for this institution."

Madam Walker usually responded by instructing Ransom to send them amounts that seemed appropriate. By 1916 she explicitly asked the office staff "to turn all begging letters over to Ransom, instructing him to "explain to them that my obligations are many and varied. It would be impossible for me to help all, no matter how worthy the cause." The same letter concluded with an addendum asking Ransom to "please send a check to Tuskegee of three hundred dollars $300.00 for the six students whom I'm helping there."

Still, the requests kept coming. In 1918, a fourteen-year-old boy named Louis Sweed wrote a letter, imploring "Dearest Madame Walker" to adopt him before he was sent to the orphanage. Having lost his mother "when a baby of two or three months" and with his invalid father "in the county poor-house," he appealed to Madam Walker, saying, "I'm sure I should love you" and begging her, "Please Please dear lady. Be a mother to me." That same year a man named F. N. Anderson wrote to Madam Walker from the notorious Angola prison farm in Louisiana where he and other incarcerated black men toiled in the sugar refinery. Writing in a neat but labored hand, Anderson asked Madam Walker to send him a few dollars. He recognized that while "you re [sic] not responsible for my mistakes in life," he noted that "i am of the negro race." He continued, "knowing your conditions in some ways that is financial [,] while I am not personal acquainte[d] with you meanwhile you a race leading clored ladie [sic]." Anderson praised Walker as "a race leading clored ladie [sic]" who was "cabler [sic] of helping some one who cant help tha self." He asked for three "or four dollars" to buy "things which is real necessary to life" as an unfree prisoner forced to labor without compensation on the prison farm.

As these examples make clear, black Americans reached out to Madam Walker for help not just because she was wealthy and famous, but because they felt as if they knew her. Madam Walker's intensive travel schedule and public appearances at churches, clubs, and commencement ceremonies certainly sharpened this sense of relatability. Louis Sweed, for example, explained, "I saw your picture in a magazine and then your name in the paper, but I never would have been so bold as to write to you had I not met a lady who knew you while you were Knoxville, Tennessee. She said you were a very great and good lady and so I thought perhaps you would help me." In March 1917, one such woman wrote to Madam Walker expressing her admiration for her work. Describing herself as one of the "nut factory girls" of St Louis, she wrote: "I think your work is the most beautiful work I have ever seen" and declared "I would like very much to learn your work." She and some of her coworkers had been "out Tuesday night to your speaking" and were favorably impressed by Walker's presentation. "I hope it is not asking to [sic] much will you please give me one of your books," she asked. Explaining that she had "a boy and a girl that I would like to read to them my girl was out but my boy was atending [sic] night school I wont [sic] him to read about you and what a wonderful success you have made." For this woman, Madam Walker served as an embodiment of black achievement, a living example she could share with her children in the hopes that they would see for themselves the possibility of a brighter future.

Familiar as black America had become with Madam Walker's narrative, as closely as her story resembled the struggles, hopes, and aspirations of their own, and as ubiquitous as her image was in black newspapers as well as on the products sitting on shelves in their own homes, it is not surprising that black Americans felt a deep kinship with Madam C. J. Walker. This sense of identification transcended financial need, as a letter from a soldier in the 317th Engineers suggests. Written just ten days after the armistice brought an end to World War I, he wrote to Madam Walker to let her know just how much the men in his company appreciated hearing her speak before they shipped out to the front. "We all remember you, and often talk among ourselves of you," he wrote. "We have often spoken of you and the words of consolation which you gave us at Camp Sherman, Ohio on the eve of our departure. Those words have stayed with the boys longer than any spoken by any one that I have known or heard of," he continued. He wanted her to know that even "while under shell-fire" the "boys of Co., 'D' 317th, Engineers . . . were talking of Madam C. J. Walker and the consoling words which she gave them." He hoped that she would be able to greet them when their regiment returned to the United States. This sense of black kinship also extended beyond the borders of the continental United States to the Caribbean, where Madam Walker and Lelia had visited a few years earlier. In 1917, Madam Walker received a letter from the Caribbean political and civil rights advocate Rothschild Francis, who was, at the time, at the beginning of his career in the Virgin Islands. "I hereby venture," he wrote, "to try and awake your interest in a few young men in St. Thomas, Virgin Islands USA." He felt that "tho' not one of your acquaintants, but upon hearing of your philanthropic disposition and love for the 'Colored Race' in every clime," Madam Walker could be counted on to support his educational work "for the intellectual uplift of this community."

Madam Walker, for her part, continued to maintain her speaking schedule and her position as a leading activist and philanthropist, despite her failing health. This is especially evident in her role in the movement to save the home of the famous nineteenth-century abolitionist and civil rights activist Frederick Douglass. Though Douglass had bequeathed the house and the surrounding property, called Cedar Hill, to his second wife, Helen Douglass, a legal technicality invalidated his will, and the property was divided among all his heirs. Helen, who hoped to safeguard the property as a monument to her husband and the abolitionist movement, purchased the estate from Douglass's heirs for $15,000 in 1895 and mortgaged the property. Just before her death in 1905, she succeeded in having Cedar Hill exempted from taxation and incorporated the Frederick Douglass Memorial and Historical Association. The association, organized "to preserve to posterity the memory of the life and character of the late Frederick Douglass [and] . . . preserve the historical record of the . . . anti-slavery movement in the United States," included some of the most prominent African American men of the day. Over the next decade, the trustees of the association only managed to reduce the amount owed on the mortgage from $5,500 to $4,000 and found themselves unable to make any further inroads on the debt. Their efforts at fundraising, even with the help of Booker T. Washington, consistently failed.

At the NACW's August 1916 meeting in Baltimore, Maryland, the trustees of the Frederick Douglass Memorial and Historical Association formally appealed to the NACW delegates for help in completing the project. For the clubwomen, their part in the possible restoration of the Douglass home and property presented an opportunity to create a national monument for African Americans, one that honored a black American who had been a slave, an abolitionist, an advocate for women's rights, and the greatest black orator the nineteenth-century. Moreover, such a monument provided an opportunity for black women to push back against the proslavery mythology being memorialized across the South through the proslavery monuments installed by the women of the United Daughters of the Confederacy.

After evaluating the issue, NACW president Mary Talbert wrote that the women of the NACW decided that the time had come for them to "show [their]true worth and prove that the Negro woman of to-day measures up to those strong and sainted women of [the] race like Sojourner Truth, Harriet Tubman, Amanda Smith, Frances Ellen Watkins Harper and others who passed through the fire of slavery and its galling remembrances." The clubwomen elected a new board of trustees and an advisory board, both comprised solely of NACW members. They then took full control over the Frederick Douglass Memorial and Historical Association, promising to "wipe out the indebtedness on the home of the late Frederick Douglass and restore it to its former beauty." In the February 1917 issue of the *Crisis*, Talbert asked that February 12, the one hundredth anniversary of Douglass's birth, be the official day of nationwide contribution to the Douglass project. Insisting that children be involved in the project, she urged "every woman's club to mobilize its boys and girls." She asked the teachers of the segregated public schools to have their students observe Douglass's birthday with a program, and have each student contribute one penny toward the restoration of the home. She also asked teachers in Sunday school programs to have their students observe the holiday and contribute a penny.

By 1918, the women had raised all the funds necessary to pay the mortgage on the Cedar Hill property. At the tenth NACW biennial convention in Denver, Colorado, Talbert announced that "all deeds, mortgages, et cetera on the Douglass Home," valued at $65,000, now belonged to the National Association of Colored Women. One Mrs. S. Joe Brown of Iowa tapped her networks and raised $750 for the NACW. Delegates from the state of Illinois managed to raise $400 for the cause. Madam C. J. Walker distinguished herself again by donating $500 to the fund; this made Madam Walker the largest individual contributor to the project. The delegates burned the mortgage on the home and pointedly referred to the day of Talbert's announcement as "The Redemption," the same term used by white Southerners to celebrate the reestablishment of Democratic Party hegemony and white supremacy at the end of Reconstruction.

Madam Walker's role as the largest individual financial contributor to the most important national fundraising campaign of the most powerful black women's group in the nation solidified her place as a modern race woman. Indeed, subsequent histories of the NACW invariably mentioned Madam Walker's contribution to the campaign to save the home of Frederick Douglass. More than any other activity, the redemption of the Douglass home signified the NACW members' spirit of race pride and race unity, their ability to mobilize networks of black women and children, and their commitment to work on behalf of their people. Madam Walker's central role in this extraordinary project served as her own personal manifestation of this political perspective. In recognition of her service, the NACW leadership asked Madam Walker to light the match they used to burn the mortgage. This dramatic action, rich in symbolism, further solidified Madam Walker's status as an iconic figure.

A businesswoman, philanthropist, race woman, and celebrity, Madam Walker was, by any measure, an unparalleled success. Nearly twenty-five thousand active agents now sold Walker products across the Americas. In 1918 her annual earnings reached $275,000 (a value of approximately $4.5 million in 2019). With her characteristic prescience, Madam Walker anticipated the new craze for makeup poised to overtake American women in the coming decade; the Walker Manufacturing Company began preparing to launch a line of skin-care products, including "safe, pure, and reliable face powder" for African American women as well as "cold creams" and "some kind of a balm for the hands of those who work in the open and women who put their hands in hot water." By 1919, Madam C. J. Walker's net worth stood at $600,000 (roughly $8.7 million in 2019). She and her business manager, F. B. Ransom, agreed that the coveted "millionaire" milestone hovered just over the horizon. Madam Walker was, to put it mildly, a woman who was at the top of her game.

She was also, however, very ill. Years of hypertension, or chronic high blood pressure, had damaged her kidneys. Diagnosed with nephritis, Madam Walker now faced kidney failure. Although she continued to oversee her growing business enterprise, sending detailed instructions to Ransom with regularity, Madam Walker also tried to rest and recuperate, preserving her energy as best as she could. Still, Madam Walker's illness quickly took its toll. Her health declined noticeably in 1917, and in November of that year she checked in to Battle Creek Hospital to recover. She followed that visit up with two additional weeks in Battle Creek in January 1918. In April she traveled to Missouri to recuperate. Her health continued to decline precipitously.

In the spring of 1919, Madam Walker came home to Villa Lewaro and took to her bed. Her condition steadily worsened, and on May 24, she fell into a coma.

Lelia, having been informed that her mother was gravely ill, began making her way home from the Caribbean where she and a sales representative for the company's Latin American and Caribbean markets were touring and scouting new markets for the company. But she would not arrive in time to see her mother again.

In the early morning hours of Sunday, May 25, 1919, Madam C. J. Walker died at her Villa Lewaro estate.

Black America went into a state of mourning. Telegrams and letters poured into the home in New York and the company headquarters in Indianapolis. Many of the condolences came from leaders of prominent African American organizations. Others came from rank-and-file agents like Miss Martha Clark who expressed her condolences to Lelia Walker Robinson in a heartfelt letter, saying, "While attending the first reception given by the Hairdressers Union of Wilmington Del; Mme Walker stopped with me, and even though she was only here a short time I learned to love her. She was so motherly and sweet, that my mother as well as myself fell deeply in love with her. Being thrown in such close contact with her; the news of her death was an awful shock to me, and indeed very keenly felt. It was only on March 26th that she was here." Offering her deep sympathy for Lelia's loss, Clark concluded with a prayer for "God [to]bless you and guide you in carrying on your great undertaking."

The nearly four dozen employees of the Madam C. J. Walker Manufacturing Company sent a signed resolution to Lelia Walker Robinson testifying to Madam Walker's role as an "absolutely just and equitable" employer, who "did not gain her wealth by overworking or underpaying her employees" but rather ensured that "they were among the most humanely treated and the best paid of the country." As these remarks suggest, Madam Walker had set a high bar for Lelia Walker Robinson, the presumptive new head of the company, to meet. For, as they put it, Madam Walker offered a favorable contrast with some of the era's more famous white captains of industry. Madam Walker "did not go about giving large donations while her employees worked under unfavorable conditions. . . . In her establishment no employee was ill at ease when the employer appeared and there was absolute co-operation between employer and employee. She [was] devoted to her helpers and so were they to her." They concluded by offering their "greatest sympathy" and pledging their "loyal support at all times and on all occasions" to their new employer, Lelia Walker Robinson.

On the Friday after her death, one thousand mourners from around the country traveled to Irvington-on-the-Hudson to pay their respects to Madam C. J. Walker. Family members, Walker agents, entrepreneurs, professionals, and entertainers arrived at the premises, taking their seats in Villa Lewaro's grand hall alongside NAACP, NNBL, and NACW officers. In addition to a portrait of Madam Walker herself, an image of "Beautiful Villa Lewaro" graced the memory book handed out during the service commemorating Madam Walker's life. Lelia and Mae, still en route home from the Caribbean, did not arrive in time to join the distinguished mourners or join the solemn motorcade to Woodlawn Cemetery in the Bronx.

A few days later, Lelia Walker Robinson held a private ceremony at her mother's graveside.

In the immediate wake of Madam Walker's passing, the Madam C. J. Walker Manufacturing Company issued a press release about the woman and her company. It concluded with the official, oft-repeated narrative of Madam Walker's life:

> The remarkable story of how Madam Walker massed [sic] a fortune in less than a decade, is one of the most striking in the history of any race. She was born in Delta Louisiana in 1867, her parents being Owen and Mattie Breedlove. She was left an orphan at the age of seven, and was taken to the home of an older sister. At the age of fourteen she married, only one child resulting from this union. She was left a widow in Mississippi at only twenty years of age and moved to St. Louis in order to educate her daughter, an advantage that she had been denied. In St. Louis Madam Walker found employment as a laundress chiefly, and according to her own story, she never allowed any woman to do her work better than herself. After many years she discovered a preparation for the growth of hair and convinced of its value, she began the sale of her goods. After a time she moved to Denver where she was more successful and from where she began to travel and introduce her preparation. She later became established in Pittsburg, and by this time was well on the road to success. In 1909 she moved to Indianapolis, where she soon opened the present factory, from which she has often derived a monthly income of more than $30,000.

This is how the girl born Sarah Breedlove wanted to be remembered, and this would be the figure that black America celebrated for decades. Madam C.J. Walker: the black woman who fashioned herself into an American icon.

~

Epilogue

Like other icons, Madam C. J. Walker remained culturally relevant long after her death. Most immediately, her legacy lived on in the name and activities of her daughter, Lelia Walker Robinson. Shortly after her mother's death, Lelia changed her first name from Lelia to A'Lelia and embarked on her own campaign as a celebrity. Referred to as the "Joy Goddess of Harlem" by the Harlem Renaissance writer Langston Hughes, A'Lelia Walker Robinson maintained her mother's tradition of hosting parties, promoting black luminaries, and creating news for the society pages of the black press. A tall, striking woman with a penchant for entertaining during a decade when adventurous Americans craved access to Harlem nightlife and proximity to black artists and intellectuals, A'Lelia became known for the Dark Tower literary salon and the lavish soirees she hosted in her Harlem townhouse. In crafting a role for herself as a Harlem host and patron of the arts, the stylish A'Lelia Walker embodied and modeled a type of edgy and avant garde New Negro Womanhood fit for the glory days of the Harlem Renaissance. Never failing to describe A'Lelia as the daughter of and heir to Madam C. J. Walker, commentators invariably linked A'Lelia to Madam Walker in every breathless story. In this way, Walker's influence continued to be felt by young black urbanites remaking themselves in the 1920s and early 1930s.

Even after A'Lelia Walker Robinson's untimely death in 1931, the name of Madam C. J. Walker continued to resonate with black Americans. Madam Walker's contributions to an array of black institutions ensured that her name remained embedded in the fabric of black institutions and celebrated by members of African American community organizations. As Elizabeth Lindsay Davis put it in her official history of the National Association of Colored Women, "The influence of this great woman [Madam Walker] will never die. Not only in life did she generously aid individuals and institutions, but in death by the provisions of her will, does her generosity still influence almost every phase of our race life and institutions." And despite the fact that African American women now had an expanded array of hair and cosmetics brands from which to choose, black women continued to purchase products from the Madam C. J. Walker Manufacturing Company for much of the twentieth century. Indeed, in the decades immediately after Madam Walker's death, the company expanded its reach and its range of products. Given the significance of the institutions supported by her philanthropy, the continued success of the company that bore her name, and the popularity of the products that displayed her photograph, Madam Walker's name and image remained recognizable to African Americans for decades.

Madam Walker was so important, in fact, that white-owned companies sought to copy and capitalize on her legacy. The white-owned Memphis-based Hessig-Ellis cosmetics manufacturer certainly understood the power of Madam C. J. Walker's career trajectory and community engagement. In the 1920s, Hessig-Ellis created a fake company employing thirty-five African Americans, trademarked the name "Golden Brown," and invented a backstory for a fictious founder named "Madame Mamie Hightower." Advertisements for Golden Brown's face powders and creams featured a photograph of a black woman captioned Madam Mamie Hightower and highlighted her commitment to race pride and uplift. This was a shameless rip-off of Madam C. J. Walker's life story, a cleverly calculated effort to tap into black Americans' collective sense of pride in Madam Walker's rise to frame as well as their continued commitment to black institution-building and philanthropy. It was also a tacit admission of the groundbreaking nature of Madam Walker's marketing strategy. Was there a woman named "Madame Mamie Hightower" anywhere in the company? Sort of. Mamie Hightower was the wife of Zach Hightower, the janitor for the Hessig-Ellis factory.

If white cosmetics manufacturers seemed to grasp—in part—the popularity of Madam C. J. Walker, African American intellectuals certainly fully comprehended the political significance of her life story. From the time of her death through the 1950s, black public historians celebrated Madam Walker's business success and philanthropic spirit. In a piece simply titled, "A Great Woman," the Crisis eulogized Madam Walker and praised her for "transform[ing] a people in a generation." With her simple "recipe" for healthy hair, Madam Walker taught "thorough and periodic cleansing of the scalp and hair, careful drying and oiling and dressing with hot 'curling' irons.

The latter part of the method," they wrote, "was the least important or neces-sary." The "essential part, cleansing and brushing," however, "revolutionized the personal habits and appearance of millions of human beings. Madame Walker made and deserved a fortune and gave much of it away generously. She deserved well of the world, and may her rest be Peace."

Published works of history by black Americans similarly praised Madam Walker as a dedicated race woman and philanthropist, a symbol of the progress of the race, and a high-achieving black "first." As the foremost busi-nesswoman of the race and the richest black woman in the world, Madam Walker was characterized as a historic figure that all black Americans should know and remember. We can see this most clearly in the collective biog-raphies published in the early twentieth century. In volumes such as these, Madam Walker invariably earned a celebratory entry.

Take, for example, the revised and enlarged edition of J. L. Nichols and William H. Crogman's *Progress of a Race, or the Remarkable Advancement of the American Negro: From the Bondage of Slavery, Ignorance, and Poverty to the Freedom of Citizenship, Intelligence, Affluence, Honor and Trust.* Published in 1920, just one year after Madam Walker's death, the authors dedicated the volume to those who sought to "read and learn, and thus come to a whole-some understanding and appreciation of what has been accomplished" by people of African descent in the United States, "in spite of the handicap" of racism. Amid scores of entries on pioneering black figures past and pres-ent are two entries on Madam C. J. Walker. The first is included in a longer entry entitled "Club Work Among Negro Women," written by Margaret Murray Washington, the widow of Booker T. Washington. Along with her synopsis of the history of the National Association of Colored Women, Washington included brief biographies of women such as Mary Talbert (the NACW president at the time of the volume's publication), Rosetta Sprague (the daughter of Frederick Douglass), Frances Ellen Watkins Harper, Mary Ann Shadd Cary, Fanny Jackson Coppin, Mary McLeod Bethune, and Charlotte Forten Grimké. Washington's biography of Madam Walker reiterated her professional history and framed her as the ideal clubwoman. By placing Madam Walker in the company of these esteemed black women with decades of activism and community engagement, Washington solidified Madam Walker's status as a clubwoman of note. Moreover, as Washington told it, Madam Walker embodied the epitome of the "lifting as we climb" motto of the NACW:

Madam Walker, as she was known to her club friends, was, at her death, which occurred only a few months ago, worth a million dollars. She began her busi-ness, that of a beauty specialist, fourteen or fifteen years ago, with no capital worth speaking of. In fact, the first earnings with which to begin her work were made at the most ordinary work. Club women everywhere rallied to her, and she with her indomitable will and faith in herself went up the ladder by bounds.

Her real estate is valued at more than eight hundred thousand dollars, besides stocks and bonds. Her factory and laboratory at Indianapolis is said to be the most complete of its kind in the United States.

Madame Walker traveled in every State in the Union, also in Cuba, Panama and the West Indies. She carried the spirit of the club wherever she went. She was always a conspicuous personage at the national gatherings, and gave liberally to the work of the association.

She led in the contributions for the purchase of the Douglass home. She was truly a product of the club work.

Madame Walker established a school in Africa and provided for its upkeep. No woman loved her own race more than she did, and no one had such abiding faith in the final triumph of the womanhood of her race through its organized efforts.

Even as she took pains to claim Madam Walker as a clubwoman, Margaret Murray Washington also placed her in the context of the era's black businesswomen. An entry on Annie Turnbo Pope Malone immediately followed Washington's biography of Madam Walker. "Mrs. Malone is also a beauty specialist," Washington wrote. "She has her fifty thousand dollar factory in one of the best localities." And an entry on the banker Maggie Lena Walker followed them both.

Having her biography included in volumes narrating black history and celebrating black progress in the Americas ensured that Madam Walker retained the status of an iconic black figure, one that editors like Nichols and Crogman hoped could serve as inspiration to the next generation. But it also meant that others were now chiefly responsible for defining the meaning of the Madam C. J. Walker story. In fact, we can see evidence of new narratives about Madam Walker emerging in the second Madam Walker entry in *Progress of a Race*. Included in the final section of the book, entitled "Who's Who in the Negro Race," this bio contains much of what had by then become familiar Walker lore. At the same time, however, the entry also contained a description of Madam Walker's origin story and product that neither she nor many of the women who used it would likely have preferred for themselves just a short time earlier. According to the brief biography, "It was while she was over her washtub engaged in the grim business of making a living, that an inspiration came to her, one which she was not slow in capitalizing. It is said that she dreamt of a formula whereby human hair could be made to grow and become straight. The formula was prepared and she experimented on herself and daughter. The result was satisfactory, so far as she was concerned, and she undertook to convince the world of the efficacy of her preparation."

Although she would likely have appreciated the inclusion of her biography in the volume, Madam Walker would certainly have taken issue with this description of her product. The entrepreneur who had taken such great pains to disseminate a carefully crafted narrative about her life and her products would have likely been surprised to see how her life's work was now being reimagined. Madam Walker was unable to control her narrative in death, and her life story, brand, and products took on new and ever-changing meanings as the United States underwent its own profound series of political and cultural changes during the last half of the twentieth century.

During the 1940s and 1950s, in the midst of the classic campaigns of the civil rights era, Madam Walker continued to be lauded as an exemplary black figure, one who African American women and men alike should emulate. She was a "black first"—a symbol of race pride. By this period, she was regularly (and erroneously) referred to as "the first black millionaire," a term that many Americans continued to ascribe to her into the early twenty-first century. Madam Walker's ability to overcome adversity and rise to great heights despite persistent and violent forms of antiblack racism served as an inspirational tale for those black Americans looking for role models. Her commitment to philanthropy was instructive, something that African Americans across class lines continued to value in the middle of the twentieth century.

For the black beauticians (as they began calling themselves by the 1930s) who followed in her footsteps, Madam Walker's commitment to black women's health and well-being, community engagement, and activism served as an iconic example for them to emulate in their own approach to beauty culture. As the historian Tiffany Gill has shown, black beauticians remained essential to various forms of civil rights activism in the twentieth century. Whether they were using their position as community leaders to engage local politicians, providing spaces for activist women to share information, traveling abroad to engage the African diaspora, raising money for organizations, or simply providing spaces to care for and restore exhausted young activists in the midst of civil rights demonstrations, twentieth-century black beauticians understood their role in the terms that Madam Walker had first established: Theirs was not frivolous work. This occupation benefitted the entire race.

Moreover, these beauticians—whether they were trained in the Walker system, Annie Turnbo Malone's Poro method, or one of the other schools that now dotted the landscape—black beauticians employed an art that Madam Walker and her contemporaries had pioneered. As they saw it, modern hair culturists extended the work that Madam Walker first began and, in the process, opened up new doors both for themselves and for others. As the *Beauticians Journal and Guide* put it in March 1951, Madam Walker's life story "is one of the great romances of modern times." Madam Walker "rose from a cabin to a castle" and "became Sepia America's Cinderella, not so much because she was born beautiful, but because of the beauty she added to the lives of others." Madam Walker "found her prince charming not so much because her feet fit the prince's glass slippers, but because she put millions of other women on their feet and enabled them to buy their own glass slippers." Now, "not only do thousands of Negro women find economic emancipation through beauty culture, but the personality of millions of people was upgraded because madame Walker lived." In language typical of midcentury America's interest in Freudian psychoanalysis, the piece proclaimed that Madam Walker's "developments constitutionally fortified the psychology of Negro women, then improved their personality and raised their ego. In this, Madam Walker's contribution has been epochal." As beauticians, they, through their training and scientific expertise, continued to engage in this important work.

Of course, as with most beauty trends, Walker products did not remain the symbol of modern black beauty forever. A few generations later, the daughters of women who had first brought the Walker system of products into their communities in the 1910s would turn their attention toward new products that heralded the scientific possibilities of the twentieth century. By the middle of the twentieth century, both black and white women spent their dollars on permanent hair altering salon treatments. Then, just a few years later, long-standing beliefs about what, exactly, defined the parameters of ideal black beauty shifted dramatically as "soul style" came into vogue for black radicals, intellectuals, artists, and college students. During the 1960s, when short and long Afros began to be seen as the epitome of black beauty and the preferred sartorial expression of one's political awareness, all methods of black hair care that altered the natural curl pattern came under scrutiny and were subject to criticism. Much as they had been in the nineteenth and early twentieth centuries, debates over how black women wore their hair became bound up in anxieties about internalized antiblackness. In the midst of this context, Madam Walker's contributions once again seemed suspicious. And Madam Walker's methods—along with the chemical straighteners developed and popularized long after her death—appeared to confirm the worst fears about the costs of self-loathing and assimilation.

Still, even in this context, Madam Walker herself remained an icon, a woman who could be celebrated for a range of contributions and personal qualities, depending on the audience. Outside the United States, for example, Madam Walker remained a black style icon. Letters from the Caribbean to the Madam C. J. Walker Manufacturing Company praised Madam Walker and her products for decades. Extraordinarily, these writers often addressed "Madam Walker" as if she were still alive. Meanwhile, in the United States, the 1980s and 1990s saw a resurgence of interest in the Madam C. J. Walker story. Amid a growing interest in black entrepreneurship, philanthropy, and women's history, Madam Walker emerged as a foremother whose life experiences and achievements anticipated the hopes and expectations of black Americans in the post–civil rights era.

Now, in the early twenty-first century, as a new generation of young black women have embraced a new natural hair movement, Madam Walker's story has a new resonance and relevance. Like Walker agents, young black women have created their own ways of sharing innovative approaches to hair care and information about new products. Rather than going door-to-door as Madam C. J. Walker and her agents did a century ago, young twenty-first-century black women use social media and digital platforms to share tutorials. Using themselves as an example, they record themselves demonstrating their methods and offering advice on how to care for curly, coily, or kinky hair and post the recordings on internet platforms like YouTube. Much like the backyard and kitchen demonstrations in Madam Walker's day, these women go on to hold conversations with viewers in the comments section of each video. Those with the most subscribers also sometimes become independent agents of sorts, trying out various products at the behest of companies seeking to expand their market reach and even offering discount codes for potential consumers.

Like Madam Walker, this new generation of women emphasize health and self-care over anything else. They characterize the move to natural hair as a way to combat the ill effects of the twenty-first century and as a more healthful alternative to other hair care practices—most notably weaves and chemical relaxers—that might damage some black women's hair. Often, these women make a point to emphasize the natural ingredients of a product. And a persistent refrain across these internet tutorials is that care of the hair must be an overall part of a twenty-first-century black woman's care of the self. Whether they realize it or not, these women have embraced a Walker-esque vision of black women's beauty culture, one where health and (in this case virtual) community take center stage.

Moreover, a new generation of black entrepreneurs have also taken Madam Walker's story to heart, marketing their own products using themes straight out of Madam Walker's playbook. The women behind twenty-first-century brands such as Camille Rose Naturals, Carol's Daughter, and Miss

Jessie's stress their own battles with hair health and their trial-and-error method of creating new formulas, reframing Madam Walker's "washtub to the boardroom" narratives as twenty-first-century "mompreneurship" or black capitalism. All of the founders of these companies place the story of their company's original founder and product creator at the center of their marketing narrative. Each of these narratives, like Madam Walker's, centers the story of a woman who, to address a hair-related problem in her own life or the life of her daughter, first began experimenting with ingredients in her own home before creating her own line. These narratives remain central to each brand's appeal, as the products use the name of the woman or place her in relation to members of her family.

As these developments suggest, the figure of Madam Walker continues to resonate with a wide swath of the American public. A new generation of fans—whether viewers of the 2020 Netflix series loosely based on her life, black "mompreneurs," or natural hair gurus on YouTube—invest meaning in Madam Walker's career trajectory and success. One hundred years after her death, the story of Madam C. J. Walker continues to live on.

~

A Note on Sources

The Madam C. J. Walker Papers at the Indiana Historical Society are instrumental for any study of Madam Walker. So too is the Madam Walker and A'Lelia Walker family archive maintained by Madam Walker's great-great-granddaughter A'Lelia Bundles.

There are several biographies of Madam Walker. Of these, the most comprehensive cradle-to-grave overview of Madam Walker's life remains *On Her Own Ground: The Life and Times of Madam C. J. Walker* (New York: Scribner, 2001), by Madam Walker's great-great-granddaughter A'Lelia Bundles. This biography was republished under the new title *Self-Made: Inspired by the Life of Madam C. J. Walker* (New York: Scribner, 2020). Tyrone McKinley Freeman's dissertation, "The Gospel of Giving: The Philanthropy of Madam C. J. Walker" (Indiana University, 2014) offers a thoughtful analysis of Madam Walker's philanthropic activities. For a more speculative account of Madam Walker's early life and career, see novelist Beverly Lowry's *Her Dream of Dreams: The Rise and Triumph of Madam C. J. Walker* (New York: Knopf, 2003).

In addition to drawing upon these biographies, this volume has been shaped by recent scholarship theorizing the politics of black women's beauty culture. The following texts have proved to be essential to all the chapters in this volume: Noliwe Rooks, *Hair Raising: Beauty, Culture, and the African American Woman* (New Brunswick, NJ: Rutgers University Press, 1996); Tanisha C. Ford, *Liberated Threads: Black Women, Style, and the Global Politics of Soul* (Chapel Hill: University of North Carolina Press, 2015); Susannah Walker, *Style and Status: Selling Beauty to African American Women, 1920–1975* (Lexington: University Press of Kentucky, 2007); Tiffany M. Gill, *Beauty Shop Politics: African American Women's Activism in the Beauty Industry* (Urbana: University of Illinois Press, 2010); Blain Roberts, *Pageants, Parlors, and Pretty Women: Race and Beauty in the Twentieth-Century South* (Chapel Hill: University of North Carolina Press, 2014). For scholarship that places Madam Walker in the context of the larger history of the rise of the beauty industry in the United States, see Kathy Peiss, *Hope in a Jar: The Making of America's Beauty Culture* (New York: Metropolitan Books, 1998).

Chapter 1

In addition to relying upon the biographies by Bundles and Lowry, the following sources offered insight into the larger context shaping Madam Walker's family history during slavery and immediately after emancipation in Reconstruction-era Louisiana.

On the expansion of slavery, capitalism, and the impact of the domestic slave trade, see Walter Johnson, *Soul by Soul: Life inside the Antebellum Slave Market* (Cambridge, MA: Harvard University Press, 1999); Walter Johnson, *River of Dark Dreams: Slavery and Empire in the Cotton Kingdom* (Cambridge, MA: Belknap Press, 2013); Ira Berlin, *The Making of African America: The Four Great Migrations* (New York: Viking Penguin, 2010); and Edward E. Baptist, *The Half Has Never Been Told: Slavery and the Making of American Capitalism.* (New York: Basic Books, 2014).

On the folk customs and practices of the enslaved, see Charles Joyner, *Down by the Riverside: A South Carolina Slave Community* (Champaign: University of Illinois Press, 1984) and Sharla M. Fett, *Working Cures: Healing, Health, and Power on Southern Slave Plantations* (Chapel Hill: University of North Carolina Press, 2002). For information on African-descended beauty rituals in the context of slavery and emancipation, see Stephanie M. H. Camp, *Closer to Freedom: Enslaved Women and Everyday Resistance in the Plantation South* (Chapel Hill: University of North Carolina Press, 2004); Thavolia Glymph, *Out of the House of Bondage: The Transformation of the Plantation Household* (Cambridge: Cambridge University Press, 2008); Shane White and Graham White, *Stylin': African American Expressive Culture from Its Beginnings to the Zoot Suit* (Ithaca, NY: Cornell University Press, 1999). Additional context about life as a slave in Louisiana was provided by Solomon Northup's personal memoir of his kidnapping and captivity, *Twelve Years a Slave: Narrative of Solomon Northup, a Citizen of New York, Kidnapped in Washington City in 1841 and Rescued in 1853, From a Cotton Plantation Near the Red River in Louisiana* (Auburn, NY: Derby and Miller, 1853).

For discussions of the experiences of enslaved and recently freed African Americans during the Civil War and Reconstruction era, see Jacqueline Jones, *Labor of Love, Labor of Sorrow: Black Women, Work, and the Family from Slavery to the Present* (1985; rev. ed., New York: Basic Books, 2010); Leon F. Litwack, *Trouble in Mind: Black Southerners in the Age of Jim Crow* (New York: Vintage, 1999); Jim Downs, *Sick from Freedom: African American Illness and Suffering During the Civil War and Reconstruction* (New York: Oxford University Press, 2012); Tera W. Hunter, *Bound in Wedlock: Slave and Free Black Marriage in the Nineteenth Century* (Cambridge, MA: Belknap Press, 2017); Joseph P. Reidy, *Illusions of Emancipation: The Pursuit of Freedom and Equality in the Twilight of Slavery* (Chapel Hill: University of North Carolina Press, 2019). Leon Litwak, *Been in the Storm So Long: The Aftermath of Slavery* (New York: Vintage Books, 1980) remains an indispensable text.

Chapter 2

In addition to the Bundles, Lowry, and Freeman biographies of Madam C. J. Walker, this chapter utilized a range of scholarship.

The scholarship on the Reconstruction era and the rise of the Jim Crow South is vast. Key works include W.E.B. Du Bois, *Black Reconstruction* (1935); Eric Foner, *Reconstruction: America's Unfinished Revolution* (New York: HarperCollins, 1988), Henry Louis Gates Jr., *Stony the Road: Reconstruction, White Supremacy, and the Rise of Jim Crow* (New York: Penguin, 2019); Stephen Hahn, *A Nation under Our Feet: Black Political Struggles in the Rural South from Slavery to the Great Migration* (New York: Belknap, 2003). Litwack's *Been in the Storm So Long* and *Trouble in Mind* were especially helpful for providing context on the history of violence in the region.

The scholarship on African American migration and labor in the late nineteenth and early twentieth centuries is equally vast. James R. Grossman, *Land of Hope: Chicago, Black Southerners, and the Great Migration* (Chicago: University of Chicago Press, 1989) remains a classic text on the history of the Great Migration. This chapter was helped by Earl Lewis, "The Making of African America: The Four Great Migrations" in Joe William Trotter, ed., *The Great Migration in Historical Perspective: New Dimensions of Race, Class, and Gender* (Bloomington: Indiana University Press, 1989); Ira Berlin, *The Four Great Migrations*; and Isabel Wilkerson, *The Warmth of Other Suns: The Epic Story of America's Great Migration* (New York: Random House, 2010). On migration to St. Louis, Missouri, see Walter Johnson, *The Broken Heart of America: St. Louis and the Violent History of the United States* (New York: Basic Books, 2020). For a definitive history of the Exoduster movement, see Nell Painter, *Exodusters: Black Migration to Kansas after Reconstruction* (New York: W. W. Norton, 1992).

On Southern black women's domestic labor and leisure activities, see Tera K. Hunter, *To 'Joy My Freedom: Southern Black Women's Lives and Labors after the Civil War* (Cambridge, MA: Harvard University Press, 1997); Rebecca Sharpless, *Cooking in Other Women's Kitchens: Domestic Workers in the South, 1865–1900* (Chapel Hill: University of North Carolina Press, 2010); and Jacqueline Jones, *Labor of Love, Labor of Sorrow.*

Scholars now interrogate the politics of dress, style, and beauty culture for people of African descent in the United States. Several of these theoretical interventions are reflected in this chapter. For examples, see Shane White and Graham White, *Stylin'* and Robin D. G. Kelley, "The Riddle of the Zoot: Malcolm X and Black Culture Politics During World War II," in Robin D. G. Kelley ed., *Race Rebels: Culture, Politics, and the Black Working Class* (New York: Free Press, 1994), 161–82. Noliwe M. Rooks, *Ladies Pages: African American Women's Magazines and the Culture that Made Them* (New Brunswick, NJ: Rutgers University Press, 2004), offers an especially useful assessment of the way elite black women marshaled style. For information on the life of Mrs. Annie Turnbo Pope Malone, see Bettye Collier-Thomas, "Annie Turnbo Malone," in Jessie Carney Smith, ed., *Notable Black American Women* (New York: Gale, 1991).

For studies that examine the emergence of American consumer and leisure culture, see Kathy Peiss, *Cheap Amusements: Working Women and Leisure in Turn-of-the-Century New York* (Reprint ed., Philadelphia: Temple University Press, 1986) and William R. Leach, *Land of Desire: Merchants, Power, and the Rise of a New American Culture* (New York: Vintage Books, 1993).

Chapter 3

In addition to the Bundles, Lowry, and Freeman biographies of Madam C. J. Walker, scholarship on black women's beauty culture proved essential to this chapter. See especially Noliwe Rooks, *Hair Raising: Beauty, Culture, and the African American Woman* (New Brunswick, NJ: Rutgers University Press, 1996); Tanisha C. Ford, *Liberated Threads: Black Women, Style, and the Global Politics of Soul* (Chapel Hill: University of North Carolina Press, 2015); Walker, *Style and Status*; Gill, *Beauty Shop Politics*; Roberts, *Pageants, Parlors, and Pretty Women*. The chapter's discussion of the honorific "Madam" or "Madame" in the larger beauty industry comes from Peiss, *Hope in a Jar*. Peiss and Roberts also offer analysis of black reformers' concerns about authenticity and morality. For antiblackness in beauty advertisements, see Rooks, *Hair Raising*.

The memoir of Mamie Garvin Fields is indispensable for a firsthand description of black women's beauty and hair-care practices from the late nineteenth through the early twentieth centuries: Mamie Garvin Fields, *Lemon Swamp and Other Places: A Memoir* (New York: Free Press, 1985).

For information on black westerners, see Marne L. Campbell, *Making Black Los Angeles: Class, Gender, and Community, 1850–1917*. See the *Statesman* newspaper for information on Denver's black community at the turn of the twentieth century. See also Ronald J. Stephens, Ph.D., La Wanna M. Larson, and the Black American West Museum, *African Americans of Denver* (Charleston, SC: Arcadia Publishing, 2008). For information on migration to Indianapolis and Pittsburgh, see Wilkerson, *The Warmth of Other Suns* and Abraham Epstein, *The Negro Migrant in Pittsburgh* (1919; New York: Arno Press and the *New York Times*, 1969).

On nostalgia for the antebellum era and its place in popular culture at the turn of the twentieth century, see David Blight, *Race and Reunion: The Civil War in American Memory* (Cambridge, MA: Harvard University Press, 2001); Patricia A. Turner, *Ceramic Uncles and Celluloid Mammies: Black Images and Their Influence on Culture* (Charlottesville: University of Virginia Press, 2002); and M. M. Manring, *Slave in a Box: The Strange Career of Aunt Jemima* (Charlottesville: University of Virginia Press, 1998).

Chapter 4

For details on Madam Walker's yearly income and sales receipts, see Bundles, *On Her Own Ground*. In addition to the Bundles, Lowry, and Freeman biographies, this chapter drew upon documents found in Louis R. Harlan's indispensable *Booker T. Washington Papers* (Champaign: University of Illinois, 1974).

The discussion of the Griffin sisters was helped by Michelle R. Scott, "These Ladies Do Business with a Capital B: The Griffin Sisters as Black Businesswomen in Early Vaudeville," *Journal of African American History* 101, no. 4 (fall 2016): 469–503. The history of the National Association of Colored Women and its leaders is quite extensive. For a comprehensive history of the organization, see Deborah Gray White, *Too Heavy a Load: Black Women in Defense of Themselves, 1894–1994* (New York: W.W. Norton, 1999). See also the Mary Church Terrell Papers at the Library of Congress and Mary Church Terrell's autobiography, *A Colored Woman in a White World* (New York: G. K. Hall, 1940).

Debates on the politics of respectability, women's roles, racial uplift, and class differences within the black population of the United States have spawned a number of books over the past two decades. Those that offer an especially useful analysis of the roles of gender and anxieties about representation include Evelyn Brooks Higginbotham's *Righteous Discontent: The Women's Movement in the Black Baptist Church, 1880–1920* (Cambridge, MA: Harvard University Press, 1993); Stephanie J. Shaw, *What a Woman Ought to Be and Do: Black Professional Workers during the Jim Crow Era* (Chicago: University of Chicago Press, 1996); Kevin Gaines, *Uplifting the Race: Black Leadership, Politics, and Culture in the Twentieth Century* (Chapel Hill: University of North Carolina Press, 1996); Michele Mitchell, *Righteous Propagation: African Americans and the Politics of Racial Destiny after Reconstruction* (Chapel Hill: University of North Carolina Press, 2004); Victoria W. Wolcott, *Remaking Respectability: African American Women in Interwar Detroit* (Chapel Hill: University of North Carolina Press, 2001); and Marcia Chatelain, *South Side Girls: Growing up in the Great Migration* (Durham, NC: Duke University Press, 2015).

The scholarly literature on Booker T. Washington is vast. Biographies that were especially useful for this project include Louis Harlan's *Booker T. Washington: The Wizard of Tuskegee* (New York: Oxford University Press, 2010) and Raymond Smock's *Booker T. Washington: Black Leadership in the Age of Jim Crow* (Chicago: Ivan R. Dee, 2009).

Chapter 5

In addition to the biographies by Bundles and Freeman, this chapter drew upon the following texts.

For discussions of the changing black political landscape, see Hazel V. Carby, *Race Men* (Cambridge, MA: Harvard University Press, 1998); Martin Summers, *Manliness and Its Discontents: The Black Middle Class and the Transformation of Masculinity, 1900–1930* (Chapel Hill: University of North Carolina Press, 2004); W.E.B. Du Bois, *The Souls of Black Folk* (Chicago: A. C. McClurg, 1903); and David Levering Lewis, *W.E.B. Du Bois: Biography of a Race: 1868–1919* (New York: Holt Paperbacks, 1994). In addition to the previously mentioned texts on the Great Migration, this chapter also drew upon the essays in Joe William Trotter, ed., *The Great Migration in Historical Perspective: New Dimensions of Race, Class, and Gender* (Bloomington: Indiana University Press, 1989). In particular, see Darlene Clark Hine, "Black

Migration to the Urban Midwest: The Gender Dimension, 1915–1930," in Trotter, *Great Migration in Historical Perspective*, 127–46. For information on the history of black women's antidiscrimination lawsuits, see Barbara Young Welke, *Recasting American Liberty: Gender, Race, and the Railroad Revolution, 1865–1920* (New York: Cambridge University Press, 2001) and Sharon Wood, "Emma Lane Coger," in Erica L. Ball, Tatiana Seijas, and Terri L. Snyder, eds. *As If She Were Free: A Collective Biography of Women and Emancipation in the Americas* (New York: Cambridge University Press, 2020), 393–410. For lawsuits and entrepreneurship as activism, see Kellie Carter Jackson, "Mary Ellen Pleasant," in Ball, Seijas, and Snyder eds., *As If She Were Free*, 312–30.

On black women's intellectual work and activism, see Britney C. Cooper, *Beyond Respectability: The Intellectual Thought of Race Women* (Champaign: University of Illinois Press, 2017) and Mia Bay et al., *Toward an Intellectual History of Black Women* (Chapel Hill: University of North Carolina Press, 2015). Anna Julia Cooper's *A Voice from the South by a Black Woman of the South* (Xenia, OH: Aldine Printing House, 1892) is a classic text in this intellectual tradition. For information on black women's internationalism in the twentieth century, see Keisha Blain and Tiffany Gill's edited collection, *To Turn the Whole World Over: Black Women and Internationalism* (Champaign: University of Illinois Press, 2019). For information on the importance of African American schools and other institutions, see Imani Perry, *May We Forever Stand: A History of the Black National Anthem* (Chapel Hill: University of North Carolina Press, 2018).

On women and modernity in mainstream American culture, see Martha H. Patterson, *Beyond the Gibson Girl: Reimagining the American New Woman, 1895–1915* (Champaign: University of Illinois Press, 2005); Joshua Zeitz, *Flapper: A Madcap Story of Sex, Style, Celebrity and the Women Who Made America Modern* (New York: Three Rivers Press, 2006); Kathleen A. Feeley, *Mary Pickford: Hollywood and the New Woman* (Boulder, CO: Westview, 2016). For an analysis of the use of psychology and the roles of desire and self-identification in emergent marketing and advertising practices, see Roland Marchand, *Advertising and the American Dream, 1920–1940* (Berkeley: University of California Press, 1985).

On modern black women's sensibilities and their embrace of Madam C. J. Walker, see Alys Eve Weinbaum, Lynn M. Thomas, Priti Ramamurthy, Uta G. Poiger, Medeleine Yue Dong, and Tani E. Barlow, eds., *The Modern Girl around the World* (Durham, NC: Duke University Press, 2008). For a history of *Half-Century* magazine, see Rooks, *Ladies Pages*; Erin D. Chapman, *Prove It on Me: New Negroes, Sex, and Popular Culture in the 1920s* (New

York: Oxford University Press, 2012); and Saidiya Hartman, *Wayward Lives, Beautiful Experiments: Intimate Histories of Social Upheaval* (New York: W.W. Norton, 2019).

Chapter 6

In addition to the Bundles biography, this chapter drew heavily from documents found in the Madam C. J. Walker archives at the Indiana Historical Society. Documents from the *Crisis* magazine and the *Booker T. Washington Papers* were also referenced in this chapter.

This chapter also utilized the following works of scholarship. For information on Harlem and black New Yorkers, see James Weldon Johnson, *Black Manhattan* (New York: A. A. Knopf, 1930); David Levering Lewis, *When Harlem Was in Vogue* (New York: Vintage Books, 1982); and Saidiya Hartman, *Wayward Lives, Beautiful Experiments: Intimate Histories of Social Upheaval* (New York: W. W. Norton, 2019). Litwack, *Trouble in Mind* is quoted here on antiblack violence.

On celebrity culture, see Sharon Marcus, *The Drama of Celebrity* (Princeton, NJ: Princeton University Press, 2019) and Feeley, *Mary Pickford*. On African American celebrity icons in particular, see Nicole Fleetwood, *On Racial Icons: Blackness and the Public Imagination* (New Brunswick, NJ: Rutgers University Press, 2015). On the persecution of Jack Johnson, see Theresa Rundstetler, *Jack Johnson, Rebel Sojourner: Boxing in the Shadow of the Global Color Line* (Berkeley: University of California Press, 2012).

Epilogue

The epilogue drew upon documents found in the Madam C. J. Walker archives and the National Museum of African American History and Culture. The epilogue also quotes heavily from "A Great Woman," *Crisis* 18, no. 3 (1919): 131 and J. L. Nichols and William H. Crogman's *Progress of a Race, or the Remarkable Advancement of the American Negro: From the Bondage of Slavery, Ignorance, and Poverty to the Freedom of Citizenship, Intelligence, Affluence, Honor and Trust* (Naperville, IL: J. L. Nichols, 1920). For descriptions of A'Lelia Walker in the 1920s, see David Levering Lewis, *When Harlem Was in Vogue* and Saidiya Hartman, *Wayward Lives, Beautiful Experiments*. For the history of the National Association of Colored Women, see Elizabeth Lindsay Davis, *Lifting as They Climb* (Chicago: National Association of Colored Women, 1933). For Mamie Hightower and the story of the Golden Brown product line, see Peiss, *Hope in a Jar* and Roberts, *Pageants, Parlors, and Pretty*

Women. For the activism and politics of African American beauticians from the 1930s through the civil rights era, see Gill, *Beauty Shop Politics.* For the style politics of the civil rights and black power eras, see Ford, *Liberated Threads* and Rooks, *Hair Raising.*

~

Index

activism: of African Americans, 76–77, 80–81, 111; of beauticians, 125–26
advertisements, 51, 89; of African Americans serving whites, 52–54, 55; for agents, 82; of Madam Walker's Wonderful Hair Grower, 55; of Villa Lewaro, 100
Africa, 124
African Americans, vii–viii, x, 61, 100, 114; as activists, 76–77, 80–81, 111; advancement of, viii–xi, 23, 54, 86, 107–8; advertisements of, 52–54, 55; cultural ethos of, 61–62; diasporic perspective of, 76; education of, 23–24, 32–33, 67; employment opportunities for, 24–27; entrepreneurship of, 68; folk traditions of, 13–15; freedom and, 11–12, 39; healing tradition of, 47; independence of, 67–68; leisure spaces of, 34–35; migration of, 21–24, 30–31, 90, 97; mutual aid societies for, 23–24, 32–33; in popular culture, 51, 52–55; after Reconstruction era, 24–27; social class of, 37, 45; violence against, 12, 23, 29, 30, 50, 62, 77, 104, 105, 109; voter suppression of, 17, 19
African American women, 46, 50–51, 123–24; aspiration of, 93, 100–101; beauty culture of, ix, 36–37, 44, 54–56; community improvement with, 62; elitism of, 82; as entrepreneur, 58–59; fashion in early 20th century of, 88, 90; as New Woman, 92–93; social class of, 81–83, 89
African descent: racism toward people of, 102; rights of people of, 77; status of, 1, 47, 65; women of, 78, 92
African threading, 14
Afro, viii, 126
agents, 83, 92, 117; advertisements for, 82; from black colleges, 85–88; clubs of, 84–85; convention of, 109; independence of, 89; at Tuskegee Institute, 71; in twenty-first century, 127
agents, of Pope, 36, 41, 44
Albuquerque, New Mexico, 40
Allmon, Charles, 105–6

~

About the Author

Erica L. Ball is a professor of history and Black studies at Occidental College. Focusing on the ways African Americans have placed visual, print, and other forms of cultural production in the service of the long freedom struggle, her work explores the connections between African American expressive culture, class formation, and political activism in the nineteenth and twentieth centuries. Ball is the author of *To Live an Antislavery Life: Personal Politics and the Antebellum Black Middle Class* (2012) and co-editor, with Kellie Carter Jackson of *Reconsidering Roots: Race, Politics, and Memory* (2017). She is also co-editor, with Tatiana Seijas and Terri L. Snyder of *As If She Were Free: A Collective Biography of Women and Emancipation in the Americas* (2020).

CPSIA information can be obtained
at www.ICGtesting.com
Printed in the USA
BVHW082152230221
600886BV00001B/1

9 781442 260382